MennoFolk 3
Puns, Riddles, Tales, Legends

MennoFolk3
Puns, Riddles, Tales, Legends

Ervin Beck

Painted Glass Press
Goshen, Indiana

2022

Library of Congress Cataloguing-In-Publication Data
Beck, Ervin.
    MennoFolk3: Puns, Riddles, Tales and Legends / Ervin Beck.
    Includes bibliographical references.
    ISBN 978-0999145005 (pbk.: alk. paper)
1. Mennonite—United States—Folklore. 2. United States—Folklore.

MennoFolk3
Copyright © 2022 Painted Glass Press, Goshen, IN 46526
All rights reserved.
Library of Congress Catalog Control Number: ~~2017909819~~
International Standard Book Number: 978-0-9991450-2-9
Printed in the United States of America
Cover design by Jenae Longenecker, featuring "Rembrandt Mennonites on Holiday" by Don Swartzentruber © 2002

Painted Glass Press
109 Carter Road
Goshen, IN 46526
paintedglasspress.com

· CONTENTS ·

INTRODUCTION ·	The Gordon Factor	1
ONE ·	Defining Mennonite: Puns and Riddles	11
TWO ·	Defining Mennonite: Narratives	25
THREE ·	More Trickster Tales	39
FOUR ·	Amish Slurs	51
FIVE ·	The Amish Joke Back	59
SIX ·	Dialect Stories	71
SEVEN ·	Bawdy Tales	79
SEVEN ·	Personal Legends: Formation	89
EIGHT ·	Personal Legends: George Brunk, Sr.	103
NINE ·	More Personal Legends	115
	Sources	137

"The best art . . . happens at the crossing places where tricksters are active and where different visions of community are contested."

—Magdalene Redekop, *Making Believe* (2020)

· INTRODUCTION ·

The Gordon Factor

MY GOOD FRIEND Gordon Yoder always has a new story to tell. Since he knows of my special interest in Mennonite and Amish stories, he takes the initiative in telling me his latest one. Invariably, he begins: "There was this Mennonite woman . . ." or "There was this Amish man. . . ."

Sometimes his stories make it into my collection. But, lately, more often they do not because their contents have little or nothing at all to do with recognizably Mennonite or Amish experience. So Gordon has become my best critic, since the message he implicitly conveys is that there is little that is ethnically unique in many ethnic stories. One story can be transferred from one ethnic group to another merely by changing a few details and the name of the group.

To coin a term, "The Gordon Factor" in my experience with Mennonite story-telling refers to the fact that one ethnic group borrows stories and jokes from another ethnic group, and a story-teller changes names and details to suit the context of performance.

That is especially true of *moron jokes*, which can be shaped to fit whatever ethnic group the storyteller wants to make fun of at the moment. Moron jokes easily become Irish jokes, or Polish jokes, or Newfie jokes. In the case of Mennonite and Amish folklore, generic moron jokes first became "Dumb Dutchman" jokes (referring to all speakers of Pennsylvania German) and then evolved into "Mennonite" or "Amish" jokes.

Ethnic jokes often make fun of traits that are typical of most American immigrants. Probably all immigrant groups have been penny-pinching, in order to succeed economically in a new culture. Immigrant groups are also known for freakish use of the English language, or baffling use of their own languages, resulting in the ethnic dialect joke. And immigrants have all been at least momentarily ignorant—hence "dumb"—regarding customs and understandings that mainstream Americans take for granted.

Of course, that pushes the point a bit too far, since each ethnic group does have cultural characteristics that distinguish it from other ethnic groups. Sometimes these distinctives are perceived by outsiders, who then stereotype all members of the ethnic group in that way. Whether or not the stereotypes accurately represent the group is a highly debatable question—but ultimately not the point. The point is that ethnic groups are *perceived in* stereotypical ways by outsiders, who then tell stories that highlight and reinforce those stereotypes. Folklorists regard such understandings as *folk sociology*. Since ethnic stereotypes have consequences in real life affairs—sometimes helpful, sometimes harmful—they should not be ignored but, first, understood. Following the work of William Jensen, folklorists regard outsiders' lore about other groups as *exoteric* lore.

Folklorists regard insiders' perceptions of their own group's nature and experience as *esoteric* lore. In such lore, one finds a knowledge and relishing of cultural details that may be baffling to an outsider but hilariously funny to insiders. For Mennonites and Amish, those esoteric details sometimes concern rules of conduct (Amish do not fly in airplanes) or peculiar social or religious customs (Mennonites use grape juice in communion) or regulations of costume (Mennonite women sometimes wear a special kind of head-covering). Indeed, it is in the stories that ethnic groups tell about themselves—in their esoteric lore—that one might expect to find the ethnic story or joke that is truly distinctive to that group. Jews will know the best stories about Jews. Mormons will know the best ones about Mormons. Poles will know the best about Poles. Mennonites, about Mennonites.

MennoFolk3: Puns, Riddles, Tales, Legends fulfills my quest to find truly Mennonite stories—always keeping in mind The Gordon Factor in borrowing and adapting stories told about other ethnic groups.

Secondarily, this is also a book of *Amish* stories, since if Mennonites tell stories about another ethnic group, that group will most likely be the Old Order Amish. At least, that is true of the Mennonite communities from which I gathered most of the stories in this book. My Mennonite informants were mainly Swiss-Alsatian Mennonites, near whom the Old Order Amish have also tended to settle, since both groups come from the same geographic, linguistic and cultural areas of Europe. Many of the informants' families were themselves originally members of the Old Order Amish, or Conservative Mennonite, or Amish-Mennonite, or Old Order Mennonite churches.

Unfortunately, the book contains virtually no Amish stories told by Old Order Amish people themselves. The Amish stories have come into my collection indirectly, or from print sources originating in the Amish community. To collect and study Amish stories with integrity, I would need to tape-record their narratives as told orally by them in their native dialect of Pennsylvania German. Although I have Amish friends, I do not know Pennsylvania-German and have never felt that such an approach to Amish people would be appropriate.

I do know that in the Amish dialect the word for story has negative meanings, conveying more the sense of *lie* than of fiction. Of course, that is true in many folk cultures. For instance, I vividly recall tape-recording the Anancy stories of a speaker of Belizean Creole English in the middle of the bush in Belize. While her husband told me his stories, his wife stood in the doorway, laughing and saying out loud, "Liar! Liar!" during his performance. On one level, she was passing a kind of moral judgment, since the family belonged to the Seventh Day Adventist Church, which frowned on the old, amoral trickster tales. But on a literary critical level, she was defining the stories being told as *fictional* folktales, rather than as *legends* intended to be believed.

The situation is somewhat similar in Amish cultures today. In *MennoFolk: Mennonite and Amish Folk Traditions* I cite the Beachy Amish (Amish-Mennonite) minister who said that he would never tell a story that was not true—but then proceeded to tell several stories that he believed to be historical events but that a folklorist would recognize as traditional legends. John Ruth, a Mennonite historian who has a keen understanding of Mennonite and Amish folk cultures, assumes that such moral condemnation of folktales by the Beachy Amish minister can be understood as the result of his people becoming self-consciously evangelical, and consequently less comfortable with their traditional culture, where storytellers are not officially encouraged but are known and honored in informal conversational situations. After all, Old Order Amish culture is inherently an oral traditional—not print- or media-oriented—culture, where informal narratives should thrive.

Informants who used to be Amish have told me that, indeed, informal Amish storytelling is abundant. Often it is very frank, even vulgar, in its contents, and its earthy nature cannot adequately be conveyed by direct translation into English. I noticed those tendencies in stories told me by ex-Amish people who had learned them in Pennsylvania German, and some Amish bluntness does emerge in the stories in Chapter 5 from the writings of William McGrath, a Beachy Amish leader.

So this book presents stories that Mennonites tell—about themselves and their cultural rivals, especially their Old Order Amish neighbors. I gathered most of the narratives in story-telling sessions that I led with Mennonite audiences of men and women. In the 1980s and 90s I often gave programs on Mennonite folk narratives, for adult Sunday School classes or as after-dinner programs, and then invited those in the audience to tell their own Mennonite or Amish stories, while I tape-recorded them. The transcriptions given here have been lightly edited for readability. The more vulgar, bawdy stories were told to me in private, or in small, intimate groups. The original transcripts are available in the archives at Goshen College.

Being a close-knit group, Mennonites sponsor many meetings for worship and study, hold many meetings to conduct church affairs, plan many potlucks for large-group fellowship, enjoy family reunions, and socialize mainly with other Mennonites in informal situations. Informal story-telling abounds in those contexts. People with reputations as good storytellers are admired and sought out, and preachers who use stories in their sermons are the most popular. In Chapter 4 of *MennoFolk* I documented one urban legend passing through a storytelling network that began at the top of the Mennonite church hierarchy and very quickly spread through grass-roots members of the church.

The stories in this book come mainly from middle-aged and older people. When I presided over a few similar programs with audiences of Mennonite young people, the results were different. The stories I told were met with less response and the young people had many fewer Mennonite stories to tell. At worst, that may be because the more acculturated Mennonite young people have a less clear sense of distinctive Mennonite identity. At best, it may mean that they have not lived long enough as Mennonites to perceive those cultural elements that remain distinctive to their people.

I wish I could include the names of the people who told me the stories, but it was impossible for me to obtain permission from so many people in preparing this book. However, I always give credit to master storytellers J. C. Wenger and John L. Ruth for the stories I recorded from them. Wenger (1910-95) of southeastern Pennsylvania, and Goshen, Indiana, was the storyteller par excellence for his generation of Mennonites, and John L. Ruth, also of southeastern Pennsylvania, has become his counterpart today. Both men are known for having worn the "plain coat" when it was no longer necessary. I take that to mean, in part, that both men wanted to associate themselves with traditional Mennonite culture, which relished both inspirational and humorous stories. Many of the stories from J. C. Wenger come from a tape-recorded interview; the stories by John Ruth come mainly from a conversation with him in Goshen, Indiana, and from his plenary session at the Mennonite Church conference at Bethlehem, Pennsylvania, in 1983, which commemorated the 300th anniversary of Mennonite immigration to America.

Mennonite stories have been self-consciously promoted by a few other individuals and venues. Most notably, for many years Katie Funk Wiebe of Tabor, Kansas, wrote a column on Mennonite humor in *Festival Quarterly*, published from 1974-1996 by Good Enterprises in Intercourse, Pennsylvania. On at least one occasion, she was taken to task in letters to the editor for publishing folk narratives that offended the tastes of readers. But she knew what she was doing, and skillfully defended their role in Mennonite folk culture. Other print sources for Mennonite stories have been the periodicals *Mennonot*, published from 1993-2003 by Sheri Hostetler and Steve Mullet, and *Rhubarb*, published since 1999 by the Mennonite Literary Society in Winnipeg, Manitoba (and representing mainly Russian Mennonite culture). Elmer L. Smith published a set of "Amish Stories" in his book *Pennsylvania Dutch Folklore* (Lebanon, PA, 1960). John R. Mumaw included Mennonite items in his essay on Pennsylvania Dutch folklore in *Pennsylvania Folklife* (Spring 1960). Rolf Brednich published some Canadian Mennonite stories in *Mennonite Folklife and Folklore* (Ottawa 1977). Kyle Schlabach's *The Cow in Science Hall: A Collection of Goshen College Folklore* (Goshen, IN 1994) presents some academic folklore from a Mennonite college. I have given credit to print sources whenever I have used materials from them.

My first two *MennoFolk* books include some Mennonite narratives, none of which are repeated in *MennoFolk3*. *MennoFolk: Mennonite and Amish Folk Traditions* (Herald Press 2004) includes chapters on stories and their functions in Mennonite culture; origin stories; inter-Mennonite ethnic slurs; trickster tales; and the Mennonite use of the Reggie Jackson urban legend, along with essays on other kinds of folk traditions. *MennoFolk2: A Sampler of Mennonite and Amish Folklore* (Herald Press 2005) is not limited to narratives, but does include studies of various kinds of stories: about family history, horse-trading, homesteading, Amish powwow, Mennonite footwashing, college pranks, bedtime tales, courtship and adoption.

As with the two earlier *MennoFolk* books, here I also present folk materials from the perspective of the academic study of folklore, by using and explaining terminology, citing variants that are earlier and from other traditions, and offering interpretations based on cultural context.

The two intended audiences for *MennoFolk3* are insiders to Mennonite culture and outsiders who want to know more about Mennonites and Amish. I fear that Mennonite readers will regard *Stories Mennonites Tell* as merely a joke book, but I hope they will also appreciate the comments and interpretations that reveal how stories function in their culture.

Outsiders will benefit in the same way, but I hope that the larger contribution of this book is to expand what is known about the folklore of religious groups in the United States. Although studies of Jewish stories and humor abound, the folklore of American Protestants has been understudied and underappreciated. Mormon narratives have been collected and analyzed by William Wilson and Austin and Alta Fife. But where are the studies of folktales told by Lutherans, Methodists, Baptists, etc., today? True, the more "bounded" a group is, the more distinctive its culture will be and the more stories its people will tell in defining themselves, especially over against other groups. But, surely, despite their greater accommodation to mainstream culture than is true for Mennonites and Amish, other Protestant groups in the U.S. nurture their own more or less distinctive folk narrative traditions.

During the Counter-Reformation approximately 5000 Anabaptists were tortured, mutilated, drowned and burned to death for their Christian beliefs. The huge book *Martyrs' Mirror* (1660), which records some of those gruesome deaths, is the fountainhead of distinctive Anabaptist-Mennonite narratives. Its accounts of suffering and martyrdom for Anabaptist principles have haunted and inspired Mennonites and Amish ever since. The folk traditional nature of the *Martyrs' Mirror* narratives has not been studied, and perhaps can only be studied by someone well versed in the language of the Dutch Renaissance.

Until that happens, *MennoFolk3* will represents that ethnic-religious tradition, in the form of modest, mainly humorous, narratives that nevertheless express much of what it has meant in historical and contemporary times to be and feel like a Mennonite.

I am well aware that some readers may be surprised, or even offended, by some of the material they find here—perhaps especially other ethnic groups, women, conservatives, liberals, traditional moralists. Folklore, of course, is a cultural realm of informally transmitted, unofficial, verbal genres and customary behaviors. Folklore seldom makes it into print or formal public presentations. It thrives best in small group and intimate exchanges. It exists often as a dissenting, transgressive counterpart to formal, institutionally approved culture. My favorite example in literature is Armin Wiebe's novel of stories, The Salvation of Yasch Siemens. Yasch lives in a kind of alternative Mennonite culture, skirting many community rules and mores but prevailing by his wits and eventually, in his own way, embodying the best of a rural Manitoba immigrant community of a few generations ago. I make additional comments on the role of potentially offensive materials at the beginning of Chapter 7 on bawdy tales.

Acknowledgements

The contents of this book derive almost entirely from oral stories that other people have told me. I regret that I could not acknowledge most of them by name. On the other hand, some might not have wanted their name attached to their story/s in print! I hope they recognize their stories, and I also hope that they will be pleased to see them here. Many thanks to all of the good-humored people who unwittingly helped write this book. The book certainly counters the stereotype that Mennonites lack a sense of humor!

I am especially indebted to Don Swartzentruber, artist from Winona Lake, Indiana, for allowing me to use paintings and drawings from his "Pop-Mennonite" series, which I admire very much. The online text of this book uses one painting or drawing for each chapter. The book version reproduces only the painting "Rembrandt Mennonites on Holiday" on the cover. The drawings and paintings do not function as illustrations of the text, except in a few cases. The main function of these cartoon-like materials is to reinforce the sense of disjunction, ambiguity and cultural provocation that I find inherent in the materials of this book. Readers will give their own interpretations and responses to Swartzentruber's art. But they can check the artist's comments on and interpretations of the drawings and paintings as found on his website <http://swartzentruber.com/art-mennonite/1-mennonite-art-introduction.htm>. Their meanings derive in part from his growing-up experiences in the Greenwood Mennonite Church, an Old Order Mennonite congregation in Delaware, influenced also by his fascination with Disney cartooning. In addition, I thank:

Ann Hostetler for her cooperation in helping make this book accessible to all via *The Journal of Mennonite Writing*, and now, via Painted Glass Press. Ann and I were co-editors of the online journal. Many thanks also to Jenae Longenecker and Philip Ruth for turning the online text into a printed book.

Christian Stoltzfus, CMW assistant, for prompt, efficient, accurate posting of the text online.

The family of Ernest G. Gehman, represented by his daughter Huldah (Mrs. John) Claude of Wilmington, NC, who gave permission for me to use their father's anecdotes about George Brunk, Sr. in Chapter 8, as originally published in the periodical *Sword and Trumpet*. Those materials are in the public domain, but I thank Huldah for her interest.

Various publishers who read the manuscript and liked it, but found the contents too esoteric for a general reader. I understand. But that is exactly why I made the book—in order to preserve ephemeral artifacts of a Mennonite-Amish culture of a certain era that is rapidly succumbing to mainstream interests and tastes.

And to all of my friends and colleagues who have encouraged me, since about 1975, to pursue my interest in the academic study of folklore and folk arts. Folklore has low status in the academy. But I agree with Raymond Williams, a founder of the Cultural Studies movement, who famously declared that "culture is ordinary."

· ONE ·

Defining Mennonite: Puns and Riddles

THE QUEST for authentic Mennonite narratives will actually begin with names, puns and riddle-jokes. Most riddle jokes do embody highly condensed narratives. But my thesis is that these elementary, gnomic forms of folklore are inherently more fixed—and least subject to alterations, variants and The Gordon Factor—than are other kinds of folklore. Consequently, they constitute more distinctively Mennonite ethnic lore than do most narratives.

By common consent, puns are the lowest form of humor. We groan first, and then laugh. Puns are so easy to create—usually spontaneously—that they enter everyday conversation as interruptive non sequiturs. We are subject to the good and the bad—to too many too often. Usually they are *nonce* words, recognized and enjoyed in a moment and then forgotten and not passed on.

One folklore genre that preserves puns, and even capitalizes on them, is the riddle-joke, which is probably the most widespread folk expressive form circulating in American culture today. Like the *true riddle* found in "primitive" cultures, a riddle-joke consists of a question that the interrogated can answer only if he or she has heard the answer before. In successful riddling, questioners must answer their own questions. Riddles are "traditional questions with traditional answers," that is, they are not created on the spot, but are memorized from prior transmission. Although true riddles exploit metaphors, riddle-jokes usually exploit puns, or double meanings, of individual words or phrases—whether in the question or the answer, but usually in the answer.

For instance, the query, "Why don't they hire Mennonites at the Kennedy Space Center?" requires the answer, "Every time they announce 'Launch,' the Mennonites run for their lunch pails" (*Rhubarb* Summer 00, p. 6). The question is rather absurd, the answer cannot be figured out, and the answer exploits the pun of *launch/lunch*.

In the range of ethnic humor, riddle-jokes play an important role because they tend to be the form that reveals the most about a group's identity and obsessions. Longer, more complex, joking ethnic narratives can often be transferred to other ethnic groups by changing minor details—sometimes, as with moron stories, just the name of the group. Although riddle-jokes are not as "fixed" in their form as are proverbs, the questions and answers of riddle-jokes are so brief and focused as to be virtually unchangeable. And the answers tend to depend on the punning use of words whose special, in-group meanings cannot be fathomed by outsiders to the group.

The *lunch/launch* joke above, of course, is merely a moron joke from American mainstream culture applied, in this case, to Mennonites, who are probably no more or less concerned about eating lunch than are other people. For this chapter I have excluded jokes like the *launch/lunch* riddle, because they reveal little that is distinctive about Mennonites. Instead, I have chosen riddle-jokes that are based on in-group humor—usually the specialized use of words in puns—or riddle-jokes whose points seem very closely related to the self-perceptions held by Mennonites or to the perceptions that non-Mennonites have of them.

Mennonite readers should "get" all the jokes without difficulty. They may want to skip the comments on individual items. But for non-Mennonites I add culturally esoteric information that will explain what is funny to Mennonites. The comments should enhance, not ruin, the humor. The sequence of the riddle-jokes presented here moves from the sublime to the ridiculous, that is, from jokes based on deeply held religious beliefs to jokes dealing with more frivolous aspects of Mennonite culture.

Nonresistance

Historically and still today, descendants of the Swiss and Dutch Anabaptists have usually taken a pacifist stance in regard to war and human relations. They are *conscientious objectors*—reviled as "C.O.'s" during national crises. Mennonites in early America referred to themselvesd as *verlosen*, or defenseless, Christians. In fact, a small group of Mennonites once named themselves the "Defenseless Mennonite Church." Until after World War 2 Mennonites tended to refer to themselves as *nonresistant* Christians. They tended to avoid the term *pacifist* because it was associated with secular politics, although today that term is an unselfconscious part of Mennonite discourse.

Mennonite groups vary in the way they apply their pacifism to public affairs. The most conservative groups refrain from political involvement, do not comment on public affairs and quietly accept alternatives to military service. The most liberal groups resist Selective Service and practice nonviolent resistance in public affairs. The most evangelical groups are more likely to accept noncombatant service, or even military service.

The first riddle-joke implies that Christian pacifism is the single most important identifying characteristic of Mennonites as a religious ethnic group:

> What are the four shortest books ever written?
> *The Polish book on How to Improve Your I.Q.*
> *The Jewish book on Work Ethics.*
> *The Black book on Real Estate Management.*

The Mennonite book of War Heroes.

Like much ethnic humor that comments on other ethnic groups, the joke exploits stereotypes and seems discriminatory and even racist. The joke has an obviously positive Mennonite bias, since the first three titles have negative implications, but the Mennonite title is based on a positive Mennonite self-perception. The joke must have been created, or adapted, by a Mennonite and it circulates widely in variant forms in Mennonite circles. For instance, one variant concludes with the title, *My Life as an Amish Electrician*, which is a slur against a rival Anabaptist group.

> Have you heard of the most extreme Mennonite pacifist?
> *He even refused to wrestle with his own conscience.*
> (*Rhubarb* Summer 2000, p. 6)

> Why did the Mennonite pacifist move to the city?
> *Because he heard the country was at war.*
> (Katie Funk Wiebe, *With* July-Aug. 1985, p. 17)

> What do you call a Mennonite nurse who faithfully follows the doctor's order while giving shots to patients?
> *A conscientious injector.*
> (Wiebe, 17)

> Why aren't American Mennonite women allowed to wear sleeveless dresses?
> *They aren't supposed to bear arms.*

Several generations ago, rather strict clothing regulations affected women in many Swiss-Alsatian churches, but less so in Dutch-Russian groups. Today dress regulations are enforced only by the Amish and the most conservative Mennonite groups. "Liberated" Mennonites tell this joke as a way of ridiculing those outmoded restrictions.

Some Cultural Traits

What is the only time when Mennonites raise their hands?
When they hang out the warsh.

This joke assumes the tendency today in some charismatic churches to raise hands toward heaven while singing or praying. Mennonites, who have historically been very restrained in emotional expression during worship services, have tended to resist these charismatic practices. The joke stresses the practical concern for cleanliness among Mennonites and ridicules some Mennonites' peculiar pronunciation of *wash* with an intrusive *r* sound—which is actually a Midland regional dialect pronunciation unrelated to being Mennonite. Except for the most conservative Mennonite and Amish groups, most Mennonites use clothes dryers today.

Mennonites' obsession with cleanliness and frugality dominates the following riddle-jokes:

Why did it take four months for the Mennonite woman motorist to arrive in Florida?
She kept seeing signs reading "Clean Restrooms" at the gas stations.

How was copper wire invented?
Two Mennonites found a penny.
(*Rhubarb* Summer 2000, p. 6)

Although this joke probably circulates in Jewish and other groups with a reputation for parsimony, it also fits very well the reputation and self-understanding of Mennonites, who have mixed feelings about the stereotype it implies.

The principle of restraint and discipline in worship services has its counterpart in Mennonites' traditionally puritan attitudes toward sex.

How do we know that Adam was a Mennonite?
Who else, living in a garden with a naked woman, would be tempted by an apple instead?

What do you call a Mennonite coffee break?
Menno pause.

Why don't Mennonites have sex standing up?
It might lead to dancing.

This bawdy riddle-joke circulates widely in the Mennonite community, and has even made its way into the novel *My Lovely Enemy* (1983) by the distinguished Canadian Mennonite writer Rudy Wiebe.

The next two riddle-jokes take for granted that Mennonite women have historically covered their heads in worship services and even sometimes in all daily activities, following the admonition in I Corinthians 11:3-6: "Any woman who prays or prophesies with her head unveiled dishonors her head [i.e., Christ and her husband]." Dutch-Russian Mennonite women earlier wore the *kaube*, a European peasant-derived black head covering. Swiss-Alsatian women wore the "devotional veiling," or "devotional covering," a black or white net head covering, also derived from European peasant caps. Today only the most conservative Amish and Mennonite groups continue the custom, but it is well recalled by more liberal groups, who associate it with the oppression of Mennonite women by Mennonite men.

How do we know that Eve was not a Mennonite?
Because she wore no covering.

What do the Mennonite missionaries in Zaire do with extra mosquito netting?
They make coverings for Mennonite elephants.

This riddle-joke may be a variant of:

What do American Catholics do with used bowling balls?
They send them to Africa to make rosaries for elephants.

Alcohol Use

As European immigrants, Mennonites condemned drunkenness, but not drinking alcoholic beverages as such. Mennonites made wine in their homes, used it in communion services, and distilled whiskey—Old Overholt, the favorite of John Foster Dulles, being one famous example. However, with the temperance movement most Swiss-Alsatian Mennonites, especially in the U.S., became teetotalers, unlike their Dutch-Russian counterparts, who had less of a conscience against drinking. Although abstinence is still the dominant position among a majority of Mennonites, the prohibition is breaking down today, as suggested by these riddle-jokes:

What happens if you take one Mennonite fishing?
He drinks all your beer.
(*Rhubarb* Summer 2000, p. 6.)

What happens if you take two Mennonites fishing?
They don't drink any of your beer.
(*Rhubarb* Summer 2000, p. 6.

What is the difference between Lutherans and Mennonites?
A Lutheran will say "hello" to you in a liquor store.
(*Mennonot* Spring 1997, p. 19)

What's a significant ethical Mennonite dilemma?
Free beer.
(*Rhubarb* Summer 2000, p. 6)

Light Bulbs

Of the many lightbulb jokes circulating about Mennonites, I have chosen only three that seem to express distinctive Mennonite traits:

How many Mennonites does it take to change a light bulb?
Seven—one to actually change the bulb and six to complain that they liked the old one better.
(*Mennonot* Spring 1997, p. 19.)

How many Mennonites does it take to change a light bulb?
Who said anything about change?
(*Rhubarb* Summer 2000, p. 6.)

How many Mennonite Brethren [of Russian descent] does it take to change a light bulb?
Fifty. Two to change the light bulb and 48 to buy the zwiebach [bread] and borscht.
(*Christian Leader*, Nov. 16, 1982)

Amish

Swiss-Alsatian Mennonites who live near Old Order Amish communities usually have a sizeable repertoire of joking stories about the Amish, as shown in Chapter 4. Although many riddle-jokes are at the expense of the Amish, the first one is merely clever and the second one may be a near-compliment:

What do you call Amish children?
Am-lets.

Defining Mennonite: Puns and Riddles

What is an Amishman?
A fur-bearing Christian.

The "fur" apparently refers to the beard that is obligatory for any Amish man when he joins the church. If the riddle-joke casts the Amish as animal-like, then it is derogatory. But *fur-bearing* also is a pun on *forbearing*, which means "to do without" or "to hold oneself back from, esp. with an effort of self-restraint" or "to control oneself when provoked" (*Webster's New Collegiate Dictionary*). The Amish certainly "do without" many of the worldly goods that mainstream Americans covet. They practice moral and cultural "self-restraint." And as defenseless Christians they "control" themselves when provoked.

Vivid sounds and sights dominate two riddle-jokes. The first is based on the Amish use of the horse and buggy instead of the automobile. The second evokes the clothing regulations of the most conservative group of Mennonites:

What goes "Clop! Clop! Bang! Clop! Clop! Bang! Clop! Clop! Bang!"?
A drive-by shooting in Amish country.

What goes black and white, black and white, black and white?
An Old Order Mennonite somersaulting down a hill.
(*Rhubarb* Summer 00 p. 6)

Names

The jokes in this section are based on the name *Mennonite* and on institutional names created by and well known to Mennonites. Mennonite self-loathing includes embarrassment over the odd name of their religious denomination. Strangers to the tradition often need to hear the word pronounced again, and then they ask about its meaning and origin. Of course, it comes from the Dutch Protestant reformer, Menno Simons (1496-1559). Some Mennonites' embarrassment by it comes from their church being named after a very human being, Menno, which doesn't seem very Christ-like. Evangelically inclined Mennonites especially advocate changing the name of their church, so that the name itself will not impede evangelism. The decline in status of the name *Menno* is further illustrated by the fact that, except in very conservative groups, Mennonites no longer name their sons Menno, despite their revival of old-fashioned names like Noah and Eli. Ambivalence toward the name pervades the riddle-jokes that follow.

What's better than one Mennonite?
Two men a night.

How do you keep an Amish woman happy?
Two men a night.

Both of these riddle-jokes were told to me by a non-Mennonite. The second joke has such currency that Garrison Keillor used it on "The Prairie Home Companion" in 2005. These jokes trivialize the name *Mennonite* by giving it a highly sexualized meaning. Many non-Mennonite tellers of the second joke probably regard the Amish and the Mennonites as the same people. But, to a Mennonite, a sexual liaison between an Amish woman and a Mennonite man evokes a kind of taboo miscegenation.

Mennonites have excelled in relief work more so than in missions. An ecumenical Mennonite institution, the Mennonite Relief Sale, is the basis of the first of two riddle-jokes that play with the meaning of "relief." Over 50 Mennonite communities in the U.S. and Canada now sponsor annual auctions and sales, at which time items donated by congregations free of charge are auctioned or sold—especially beautiful quilts—with all proceeds going to the worldwide relief efforts of the Mennonite Central Committee. In recent years the sales have raised an average of $5,000,000 per year for international charity and development. I have written about the relief sales as folk festivals in Chapter 9 of *MennoFolk*.

The first joke is based on a TV advertisement that asked, "How do you spell 'relief?'" i.e., from pain. The second joke adds scatology to the otherwise noble meaning of "relief" in Mennonite circles.

How do Mennonites spell "relief"?
S-a-l-e.
(Wiebe, 17)

What's another name for a restroom at a Mennonite conference?
Mennonite Relief Center
(Wiebe, 17)

Yoders

Because of shared national, linguistic and historical origins, both the Swiss-Alsatian and Dutch-Russian Mennonite communities, especially in rural areas, bear a predictable set of family names. The Amish, who have always been separatists, represent this tendency best, since there are only about 100 different family names in their total membership of about 150,000 in the U.S. and Canada. Among Swiss-Alsatian Mennonites and Amish, the family names of *Miller* and *Yoder* predominate—Yoder being more distinctive, perhaps, since Miller is also a common name in mainstream English culture. Folklorist Don Yoder (a Lutheran) has made a detailed study of the origin of the patronym *Yoder*. Many Mennonite jokes exploit it to suggest the inbred nature of the Swiss-Alsatian Mennonite community. One joke below also acknowledges the many Swiss-Alsatian Mennonite families named *Beachy* and *Bontrager*.

Why are there no Negro Amishmen?
Because Kunte Yoder fell overboard.

Have you heard of the new Mennonite college at Shipshewana, Indiana?
It's called Yoder Dame and their nickname is "The Fighting Amish."

What would happen to the Mennonite Church if all the Yoders left it?
It would be deYoderized.

Have you heard about the confused boy whose father was Amish and mother was Japanese?
Every December 7 he attacks Pearl Bontrager.

And also these variant responses:

He started a car company called ToYoder.
Which went so well that he started another one, MitsuBeachy.

Titles

Comic titles of books, films and musical compositions are frequently set up in the form of riddle-jokes, as indicated by the one about Polish, Jews and Blacks that opened this chapter. Of the many comic titles circulating among Mennonites, a selection appears below. They come from an e-mail group mailing, "A Mennonite List of Musts," of unknown origin, but clearly originating in the Mennonite culture of the western U.S. and Canada. The humor of most of them comes from puns on common Dutch-Russian Mennonite family names, which makes them resemble the "Yoder" jokes above. One comes from a Russian and Kansas place name.

A Mennonite Reading List
Moby Dueck [doo-ek]
Of Mice and Mennos
The Old Man and the Siemens [See-mens]
Reimer of the Ancient Mariner
The Koehn [keen] Mutiny
The Hairy Epp
The Midnight Ride of Paul Regier [Re-geer]

Books for Children
Rempelstiltskin
Krahn-Tiki

Little Known Mennonite Historical Figures
Santa Claassen
Alexanderwohl [place name] the Great
Genghis Krahn
Woody Woodbecker

Miscellaneous Musical Masterpieces for Mennonites
The NutKroeker [croaker] Suite
Who Let the Schrags Out?
Hey, Hey, We're the Juhnkes [young-keys]!

In the Old Testament, Samson posed the true riddle of the honeycomb to his wife's family (Judges 14:5-20). In Greek mythology, Oedipus solved the true riddle of the Sphinx. In mainstream American culture, the riddle joke and the pun are probably the most widely circulating types of folklore. Mennonite culture, too, nurtures these universally expressive forms, exploiting different linguistic and cultural resources.

· TWO ·

Defining Mennonite: Narratives

SOME NARRATIVES serve as explicit or implicit definitions of what is meant by the designation *Mennonite*, whether in regard to cultural traits or religious commitment.

The most obvious kind of story that does this is the narrative that places a Mennonite, or Mennonites, in the punch line as the final ethnic group in a series of three or four—as with the Polish-Jewish-Black-Mennonite "book titles" riddle that opens Chapter 1. The Gordon Factor is strong in such stories, which usually communicate only a harsh, generic put-down of the final group in the series. Since they are easily transferred, by substitution, to other ethnic groups that one wants to make the butt of a joke, only one will be used here, because of the venue where it was collected.

> When the Episcopalian priest, the Baptist pastor and the Mennonite preacher boarded the plane, it was found that the Episcopalian had a relatively light bag, the Baptist had a somewhat heavier one, and the Mennonite had the heaviest. They talked and eventually came to this topic and explained what they had inside the bags. The Episcopalian said that he had four sets of underwear: one for Monday-Tuesday, one for Wednesday-Thursday, one for

> Friday-Saturday, and a clean set for Sunday. The Baptist had seven sets of underwear, one for each day of the week. The Mennonite said, "I have twelve sets: one for January, one for February, etc."

Although the story is told by many Mennonites, this version was told by Don Jacobs, a Mennonite missionary, at the church-wide assembly of Mennonites gathered at Bethlehem, Pennsylvania, in 1983. Jacobs interpreted the story in a positive light, as emphasizing the high value that Mennonites place on thrift. But surely the more obvious meaning of the story is that Mennonites are "dirty" in personal hygiene—which contradicts the normal stereotype of Mennonites as obsessed with cleanliness. Jacobs' use of the story illustrates variability depending on context. He was telling the story to Mennonites gathered decorously, expecting an uplifting message, so he gave the story the best possible interpretation for the context.

Misunderstanding *Mennonite*

Some stories that cannot be transferred to other ethnic groups concern the humor that results when people misunderstand the odd name "Mennonite," whether innocently or deliberately, as has already been seen at work in some of the riddle-jokes in Chapter 1.

The following cluster of stories will illustrate the fun that results when *Mennonite* is misunderstood:

> A non-Mennonite was walking in a town in eastern Ohio with his grandson, who saw an Amish person for the first time in his life. "Grandpa, what's that?" he enquired. "A Mennonite," the grandfather replied. "Well, what is he in the daytime?" the boy asked.

> You'd think . . . South Bend would have heard of Mennonites. The last time I was in the hospital there they had written on my intake sheet, "Menno Knight."

Americans often confuse the Amish with the Amana colonists, and Mennonites with Mormons. Mennonites are also confused with an obscure people in the Old Testament scriptures. Or maybe even with an infection or insect.

> Levi [Hartzler 1909-2002] taught this English course at Elkhart [Indiana] High School. There was something [in it] about the Midianites, and this boy was writing about it and he said, "These Mennonites."

> The Erbs of Johnstown, Pennsylvania, upon their return from Australia, reported that once when they were speaking to a civic group, someone came up afterwards and said, "I've often read about you Midianites in the Bible, but this is the first time I've ever seen one."

> [At Eastern Mennonite College] our YPCA was responsible for having street meetings in different parts of the country. There were four of us guys, and two girls. During the evening service, on the street corner, a lady accepted the Lord. And so we wanted to go to her home afterwards to make further contact, you know, and get better acquainted. So we went into this home to have a little service, and while we were sitting together there, in comes her husband. He looked around the room, spotted us guys with plain coats on, wondered who we were, sat down beside me and asked if he could tell a joke—tell a

story. It was his own home. I didn't want to say no. So he said, "A friend of mine was in the hospital in Harrisonburg and I stopped to see him one day and I asked him how he was getting along. He said, 'Oh, pretty well. The Mennonites bother me so much here.' I said, 'Oh, that's OK. Just put some powder on. Rub it in before you go to bed. They won't bother you any more.' You can imagine how we felt there, trying to make contact in his home with the lady! That helped me later on—take it with a smile!

The story lends some support for the claim that the name *Mennonite* is a hindrance in evangelism, although in an unusual way.

The bawdy pun inherent in the word *Mennonite*, discussed in Chapter 1, surfaces in narratives, too. One account is claimed to have been an actual occurrence—a slip of the tongue—although it more likely is an elaborate development into narrative of the riddle jokes:

A student who . . . grew up in Chicago decided to do a sociology report [in college]. His topic was to interview a prostitute in Chicago. And so he went in, paid his fee, and he talked with this prostitute. He asked her how many tricks she did in a particular evening. She said, "Twenty." So he came back and was giving his presentation to a sociology class. And as he was going through his presentation he came across this one question and he said that she could handle "twenty Mennonites."

It is unlikely that a Mennonite college student would have been encouraged to pay to see a prostitute for a class project.

Mennonite Ideals

From these raucous, degrading uses of the term *Mennonite* we turn to stories that embody some of the most deeply held beliefs in Mennonite and Amish communities. As will be noted, some have been made popular in Mennonite circles by John L. Ruth, a Mennonite historian of the Franconia and Lancaster Mennonite and Amish communities in eastern Pennsylvania. He told the first one in responding to my question, "What is the archetypal American Mennonite story?"

> A Mennonite man, broke, borrowed money from the bank for a business or farming venture and got a wealthy man in Lancaster County, a Mr. Ringenberger, to sign the note for him. When the loan came due, he still couldn't repay it and decided to ask Ringenberger to re-sign the note. Shortly after, and before he could approach Ringenberger, the debtor died. The bank told Ringenberger one day when he was in the bank that he was lucky the borrower hadn't got him to sign, since now the bank was responsible for the debt. "He was going to ask me to sign?" inquired Ringenberger. "Let me see the note." The teller slipped him the note, whereupon Ringenberger promptly signed it, thus taking upon himself the debt.

Ruth said he had a special "affection" for the story because it shows that Christian community is important enough to Mennonites for them to be willing to pay for it.

A second story told by Ruth defends the Old Order Amish from the charge that they do not adequately articulate their faith, in an evangelical fashion:

> A young Amish man attended a revival meeting, where he had his eyes opened to the kind of self-consciousness regarding religion that he was unaccustomed to in his unselfconscious, integrated Amish community. When he returned home, he confronted his mother: "Mother, why didn't you ever teach me these things?" And his mother broke down, crying. Only later did the young man realize that his parents and community had been teaching him those things ever since he was a little boy, in every unselfconscious thing they did.

Mennonites, too, accept the point of this story, which is that a life of Christian discipleship requires that actions speak louder than words; that Christian faith must be totally integrated into one's everyday life.

Three stories from early American Mennonite history emphasize the traditional Mennonite value of humility—of submitting to the fellowship of believers and not thinking highly of oneself.

> In Amsterdam [Dirck Keyser, Sr., 1635-1714] had been a silk merchant, and after he arrived here he wore a silk coat, which caused his neighbors some disquiet. Some of the brethren calling to talk over his worldliness found him in the garden. As he advanced to meet them he wiped his hands on his coat. They concluded, on seeing that, that he did not value it unduly, and so said nothing of the object of the visit.(Charles F. Jenkins, *Guide Book to Historic Germantown*, 1904.)

> As the bustling young Philadelphia lawyer Samuel Pennypacker, hot on the trail of his worthy "Mennonite" ancestors, saw Deacon Joseph Tyson approaching from his corn-field, he began by asking, "Is this Mr. Tyson?" "My name is Tyson," replied the deacon coolly, "But not Mis-

ter." (Ruth, "A Christian Settlement," *Mennonite Quarterly Review* (Oct. 1983)).

Many other stories support the Mennonite position of nonresistance, or pacifism, especially during a time of war.

> An ancestor of [J. Herbert] Fretz's [1921-2013] was approached by soldiers during the French and Indian war. They demanded that he give them his gun, which hung over the mantel. He agreed, but added, "I will give this to you, but I want to keep hold of the butt end."

In other words, he would keep them from shooting it by forcing them to hold the end of the barrel only.

John Ruth regaled the Bethlehem '83 audience with other accounts of historic Mennonite pacifism. Before alternate service provisions were made for conscientious objectors during World War 2, Mennonites would hire people to take their place in the army, go to jail, serve as noncombatants, or even carry guns.

> An army officer chastised Christian Good for not shooting. Good: "I didn't see anything to shoot at." Officer: "But didn't you see those soldiers?" Good: "Yes, but they're people and we don't shoot at people."

> Stonewall Jackson commented on the Mennonites and Dunkards in the Shenandoah Valley, fighting in his army: "They shoot but they don't hit anything."

> Frank Moyer of Lower Salford bought a substitute in the Civil War. When he was killed, Moyer stood over his grave and said, "That's me."

Mennonite acculturation in the U.S. during the nineteenth century included adapting religious practices from holiness and evangelical American denominations. Although revival meetings and tent campaigns peaked in the 1950s, some Mennonite churches still hold spiritual emphasis weeks. And for several years Goshen College sponsored renewal festivals, which generated this comment by a non-Mennonite observer:

> When they first started the Festival of the Spirit, Earl Gray—of course he's non-Mennonite—he said, "Yeah. I just don't understand these Mennonites. It must be like the library card. They renew their religion every year."

The relief work of Mennonite Central Committee (MCC) and Mennonite Disaster Service (MDS) enables Mennonites with practical skills to apply them to relief efforts following wars or natural disasters. In areas where MCC and MDS have worked, Mennonite ingenuity and hard work are admired.

> Paul Ruth [1903-98] was in Europe after World War 2, distributing flour. One Saturday afternoon in the Mennonite community of Westphalia, a boxcar of food arrived but was parked with its door absolutely blocked by a telephone pole. No remedy, since the crew had left for the weekend. The Mennonites were hungry. Paul took a GMC truck and with a winch inched the train forward, bit by bit, to the [German] Mennonites' great disbelief. When the train was moved enough, an old German said, "No wonder we lost the war to the Americans!"
> — John L. Ruth

Mennonite Reality

Many more joking stories expose the darker side of Mennonite life, especially the way they put their beliefs into practice. A story that emphasizes a certain kind of narrow-mindedness in Mennonite groups will introduce this broad category:

> Mennonites were having a conference and they advertised the need for housing in the community, to put up people [overnight]. So people were calling in and saying they could have one or two people stay at their house. And here a lady called in and she said, "I can take care of eight Mennonites." And the person answered, "Oh, that's wonderful. How many beds do you have?" And she said, "Just one." He said, "Well, how can you expect to get eight Mennonites into one bed? She said, "Well, I've heard they're quite narrow."

This story has also been told of Baptists and, no doubt, other Protestant groups.

Two stories from Dutch Mennonite culture emphasize the less admirable Mennonite traits of legalism and a certain kind of stubbornness, which may derive from—or at least complements—Mennonites' separatist, nonconformist stance toward the world:

> A Mennonite lived along a dike one winter [Sunday]. It was such a nice clear day so he put on his skates and skated down the dike to go to the meeting house for services. And then he got called on the carpet for skating on the Lord's Day—which was improper. He said, "I didn't skate from the joy of it. I skated to get to the service." And they said, "The crucial question is, 'Did you enjoy it?'"
> — J. C. Wenger

This one comes out of Holland during the war. I heard it in the Netherlands. It is about a Mennist Deckkop in the north of Holland. That's simply a word for a stubborn Mennonite. "The thick-headed Mennonite" would be a literal translation. During the war when the Nazis were there, they confiscated all the beef and so the Dutch people were short of meat. If they wanted beef they had to secretly kill the beef and keep the meat away from the Nazis. So they'd go out to the barn without lights so no one could find that they were there. And Jans and another guy went out one night to kill a beef and instead of using a gun (so they wouldn't be heard) they used a sledge hammer. And the one fellow said, "Well, Jans, I'm going to hold it and you hit it." And he struck it about three times, and says: "Is he dead yet?" "No, but I'm going to let him go if you don't quit hitting me over the head."

Two stories concern Mennonites' peculiar practices associated with the doctrine of non-conformity to the world and plain living, its corollary in practice. One exposes the scandalous ambiguity inherent in Mennonites' not using wedding rings. One shows that, even with wedding rings, Mennonites are suspected of unorthodox behavior.

A conservative Mennonite group went to somewhere in South America to do missionary work, and after being there several years, they learned that the local people thought they were living there without the benefit of marriage because they weren't wearing wedding rings.

At an interdenominational training for young adult ministry last summer at Lake Geneva, my counterpart June Dunn was approached by a woman who said, "I see you're wearing a wedding ring. Do Mennonites marry?" To which June answered, "Only if they want to."

Several stories concern the experience of "outsiders" when they join the Mennonite Church:

> A Mennonite pastor was serving Communion for the first time to an elderly convert. When she was given the wine, she exclaimed, "Bottoms up!"

The humor here is two-fold. Mennonites advocate abstinence from alcohol and in most Mennonite communion services the "wine" is actually grape juice. The convert clearly is used to social drinking, and her exclamation should be a prayer or blessing instead.

> A convert came into the church from the Presbyterians, and after he was in a while, he started wearing a plain coat. And somebody then asked him where he got his plain coat. He said, "Oh, well, I just traded off my golf clubs to a Mennonite going the other way."

The story carries less punch nowadays since most Mennonite men have abandoned the plain coat, and Mennonites even sponsor an annual Mennonite Golf Classic to raise money for charity.

> I can tell one, but I'm embarrassed to do it. . . . You have to stand to do it. It's the story of the Mennonite man in the Franconia Conference that became a bit better off, financially, and he decided to get rid of his plain coat. He went to Hope's in Souderton where they have tailors to make suits. This was just the time when these new . . . polyesters were on the market. So he asked to have a new

suit made of this new polyester. When he took it home, the suit didn't fit very well. So he went to the tailor and said, "You know," he said, "the sleeves on this suit are much too short." The tailor said, "Well, this is the new polyester cloth. I tell you, it stretches. So all you have to do is, when you have time, just hold your sleeve down like that [demonstrates, here and throughout, constantly] and it'll soon get OK. So he would always be pulling this sleeve to get the thing to fit. But then he noticed that when he pulled down on the sleeve, the tail would come up. So he went back to Hope and he said, "Look," he said, "whenever you tell me to pull the sleeve down like this, the tail comes up, and that doesn't look right." The tailor said, "Well, you just pull down [the tail] and it'll stretch and fit." And then he noticed when he stood in front of the mirror one day—when he was pulling this way and pulling this way—that the lapels, which were sort of new to him, were all pulling away. So he went back to Hope the third time and Hope said, "Well, really, what you need to do is, when you're pulling this sleeve like this, pulling it down like that, just bring this over like this [puts chin on lapel to hold it down] and just keep stretching it. . . So he was standing down there at Main Street in Souderton waiting for his wife. He just stood there, going like this [constantly doing the three motions]. A New Mennonite couple walked by. The New Mennonite lady said, "You know, I sure pity those handicapped people." And [the New Mennonite man] said, "But do you notice, he has an excellent tailor. His suit fits perfectly!" An alternate ending: It was a Franconia [Mennonite] couple that walked past, and one said to the other, "See what happens when you throw away your plain coat."

Defining Mennonite: Narratives

If outsiders are going to regard Mennonites as peculiar people who do peculiar things, the following story shows one woman taking advantage of that stereotype:

> A Mennonite woman from eastern Canada was ready to deliver a baby but eager to avoid all the admitting procedures. When the medical officer saw her admission form, he noticed she was a Mennonite. Not knowing what that was, he thought perhaps she required special medical consideration—just as Jehovah's Witnesses cannot receive a blood transfusion. So he asked her if such was the case. She seized the opportunity and said, "Yes, I'm a Mennonite, so I can't have enemas."

Although in theology and belief Mennonites are an idealistic people, they are also eminently practical, and pride themselves on the ability to get things done—whether in everyday labor or in relief and service projects. Two stories show the practical impulse winning out, even over evangelism and romance.

> Well, this is an Illinois story. But since "Rabbi" Eigsti [the narrator's husband Orie J. Eigsti 1909-2003] isn't here, I'll tell it. I only heard it. I've never told it before. But he says the Illinois farmers were in church one Sunday and the minister had told about this cloud formation in the sky: "G P C." And the minister said, "That means <u>go preach Christ</u>!" And one of the farmers stood up and he said he had seen the formation, too, but he interpreted it to say, "Go plow corn!"

This story illustrates both Mennonites' suspicion of supernatural manifestations and a reluctance to do mission work.

> A Mennonite woman was reading Maribell Morgan's book, *The Total Woman*, about how to please your husband and get everything you wanted. So she decided to try some of those techniques. When her husband came home from work one day, she greeted him at the door with nothing on but a big, beautiful smile, and it turned out that it worked really well for her. She was telling all her friends about the wonderful success of it. Her husband bought her a Roto-Tiller.

The story was told by a feminist-inclined college student as a way of criticizing Mennonite women who relish their traditional roles as helpmeets and domestic laborers.

With their ancient history of martyrdom, their attempt to follow literally the "hard" sayings of Jesus, their often non-conformed lifestyle, their shunning of tobacco, alcohol and dancing, their hard work, and their ethic of service—Mennonites can be perceived as holier than other Christians, or, worse yet, can so regard themselves.

> A visitor was touring central Kansas and got filled to the gills with Mennonites. First he went to Newton, then to Hillsboro and finally to Goessel, and found nothing but Mennonites. So he went into a Mennonite church. "I'm sick of Mennonites," he said. "I want to go some place where there aren't any Mennonites." "Why don't you go to hell?" said the pastor. "There are no Mennonites there."

Does that joke compliment Mennonites or satirize them for self-righteousness? The story was given national currency by being included in an article on religious humor in the *Pittsburgh Press* on July 2, 1983. A variant referring to any speakers of Pennsylvania Dutch was published by Elmer Lewis Smith in *Pennsylvania Dutch Folklore*, p. 26.

• THREE •

More Trickster Tales

THE "MORE" in the title of this chapter alludes to Chapter 4 in my first *MennoFolk* book, which studies a tradition of Mennonite trickster tales that reaches all the way back to Menno Simons (1496-1559), after whom the denomination is named. The legend about clever Menno in the stagecoach, eluding authorities by means of deceptive speech, embodies what in Dutch culture is known as "The Mennonite Lie." The trickster allows his opponent to misunderstand a speech or a situation and benefits from that situation without revealing the truth of it. The pursued Mennonite escapes danger without literally telling a lie, thereby preserving the Anabaptist-Mennonite ideal of letting "your yea be yea" in an ethnic culture that treasures clear, honest speech.

In recent years, the legend of Menno in the Coach has mutated into the legend of the Mennonite preacher, who is dressed in his "plain" coat, being mistaken for a Roman Catholic priest and given special favors or treatment. The Mennonite preacher accepts the benefit without explaining his passive deception. Most frequently, such recent versions of the legend concern the late, well-known Mennonite theologian and preacher J. C. Wenger speeding down the highway and excused by a policeman or state patrolman.

Stories of the plain-coat Mennonite preacher will dominate the second half of this chapter, but other kinds of Mennonite and Amish tricksters in the first half will suggest the rich variety in the tradition, which Mennonites seem to relish. All of the stories resonate in the context of historical and recent Mennonite confessions of faith, in which an emphasis on integrity of speech, related to the non-swearing of oaths, is the one doctrine that appears most often in Mennonite sub-groups.

Tricky Behavior

The first Mennonite trickster uses silent pantomime to imply a physical violence that he never would use in actual life. Paraphrased here, it was told to me by a Beachy Amish minister who said he would never tell a story that was not true, although his story has all the trappings of a folk legend, including three-fold action. It also belongs to the tradition of implied threat associated with the tall tales of Strong Isaac Kolb and Strong Jacob Yoder in Chapter 10 on personal legends.

> Bontrager's first ancestor to settle in Elkhart County came here through the Ohio wilderness, driving oxen that pulled a wagon full of the family's possessions. One night they camped out in the wilderness beside the road, only to find themselves surrounded by a band of hostile-looking Indians, who waited and watched. What should the nonresistant Christian do? Well, first he built a bright fire behind the wagon. Then he went to the rear axle of the wagon and lifted it once and then set it down. He lifted it a second time and set it down. He lifted it a third time and set it down. Seeing this show of strength, the Indians vanished into the forest.

In this case, The Mennonite Lie, implying brutal strength waiting to be used in violence, works better than prayer.

From the sublime to the ridiculous, we turn to the story of Mennonite ministers caught with their pants down. Or off!

Two General Conference Mennonite pastors were at a lake with members of their congregation, and they decided they wanted to go skinny-dipping. So they went all by themselves and left their clothes on the edge of the shore. All of a sudden they saw the boats with their congregation people coming, and they knew that they were going to dock right there where their clothes were. So they ran to the shore as fast as they could. Their clothes weren't right there. One of the men couldn't run faster so he put his towel around his head. The other guy says, "Well, why do you put your towel around your head?" And he said, "Well, I don't know about you, but my people know me by my face."

This is a favorite story in Mennonite circles, but is usually told about boys in a Mennonite college who, after showering, raced through a girls' dorm floor with only a towel wrapped around their heads—either because someone had hidden their clothes or because they wanted to "streak" without being recognized. The latter makes the most sense, since they could have wrapped their towels around their loins and preserved their modesty. Adapted here to two preachers at a lake, the story makes less pleasing sense because members of the congregation surely would have known who the single streaker was, even if they didn't recognize him by his private parts.

Tricky Speech

The first two stories illustrate trickery by clever deeds. The more typical Mennonite trickster is one who uses deceptive or ambiguous meanings of words to convey a false message that saves the Mennonite, either physically or morally.

E. G. Kaufman [1891-1980], past president of Bethel College [Newton, Kansas], was in New York City about to attend seminary. This was at a time when housing, particularly student housing, was very hard to come by. And many of the landlords were Jewish and would take Jewish boarding students, but not gentiles. Because of their need for separate eating quarters, I guess, Jewish students would eat with the family, but gentiles could not. Anyway, E. G. was getting pretty desperate to find a room, and finally went up and knocked at one of these Jewish families. The landlord gave E. G. a close look and wanted to know what E. G. was doing. E. G. told him he was going to seminary. (This was obviously a non-Jewish seminary.) The landlord explained that they did not rent to gentiles, and E. G. finally piped up, "But my name is Kaufman!" The landlord said, "Kaufman! Well, why didn't you say so!" So apparently E. G. got his room after all.

Here the Mennonite is more deliberately deceptive than in other trickster stories. He deliberately wants the Jew to misunderstand the "seminary" he is attending, and he knowingly emphasizes his very common Mennonite family name, which is also a common Jewish name.

With the rise of labor unions in the United States, pacifist Mennonites early on forbade members to join unions because unions ultimately will resort to coercion, even force, to attain their ends. While Mennonites were predominantly farmers, the ruling was academic, but as Mennonites moved into more urban occupations this rule created hardships, which the following story solves in a tricky way:

Some Mennonites from Kalona [Iowa] were working on a plastering crew in Iowa City, when they were approached by a union organizer. They heard this fellow say, "Do you belong to the union?" And he said, "Yes, I belong to East Union." See, that's the Mennonite church [near Kalona].

And both fellows inside [the house] also belonged. And of course this went all over the community right away. They said, "Benny, he got rid of [the union organizer] all right by telling him he belonged to East Union," and both of the plasterers belonged to East Union, too. So they were "union" men!

Historically, Mennonites have tended to be separatists in the countries and cultures in which they have lived. Often they have sought special privileges of exemption from military service and of operating their own schools in their immigrant languages. Those positions inevitably create tensions with the government. One story shows how Mennonites resolved an issue through a linguistic technicality:

The Mennonites in Brazil were told during World War II that they could not hold their services any longer in German because of the war with Germany. And the Mennonites said, "OK. If we can't use [High] German we'll use Plautdietsch [a Low German dialect]. And the government said, "You daren't use Plaut because that's a form of German, too." "No," the Mennonites said, "it's a form of Dutch." Well, you can argue both sides of that. It has certain resemblances to both languages. So the government sent a professor out to the colonies of the Mennonites in Brazil to find out what kind of a language they did speak. And he said, "How do you say horse in Plaut?" Well, the word in Plaut is Piert, which is a form of Ferde, which is the High German word for horse. But there is a word that's a little bit slangy that's about like our word nag, and it's schrog, and this German professor had never heard of it. So he said, "How do you say cow?" Well, the Low German word for cow is Ku, which is the same as High German.

But, again, there's a slangy word which would be about like you'd say in English, "the old bone pile." And it's pronounced Klem. So they said that. And he had never heard of that. So he went back to the government. He said, "The language they talk is not German." Then the Mennonites laughed up their sleeves and conducted their services in Plaut and enjoyed it more than ever.

Although the story is more often told about Mennonites in Prussia and Ukraine, this version came from J. C. Wenger, himself the hero of many, many Mennonite trickster stories. Clearly, he enjoyed the larger tradition, just as he apparently relished being a hero in others' trickster stories about him.

One Amish trickster story is based on the clever, literal interpretation of a phrase:

My mom and dad went out west one time. And Dad had a beard and when he was out west he had a close shave. That's part of the story. Then Mom had always said, "Well, she won't sleep with Dad if he shaves the beard off." But of course he did have a close shave and he lost the beard. And so I asked Mom, "How do you, well, how do you do this?" She said, "Well, I went to bed first. He had to sleep with me." I guess it's all in how we look at it! That's the way a lot of the jokes are. But I think it's good for us to laugh at ourselves and see that we are still God's people.

The story was told by a pastor of a Conservative Mennonite church, following a men's fellowship dinner at which I and members of the audience told Mennonite and Amish stories. The program was followed by religious songs by a men's quartet, after which the pastor stood to close the evening with this story, other comments and a concluding prayer. Although he appreciated and enjoyed the ambiguity of this family story, his comments implied a dichotomy between relishing funny stories and being "God's people."

Tricky Costume

Stories of the Mennonite preacher as trickster wearing the plain coat have a predictable narrative pattern, although some of them clearly derive from the actual experience of Mennonite men being mistaken for Catholic priests. John Mosemann (1907-89) was a well known Mennonite pastor who, according to his own counting, was stopped for speeding four times in his life. In each case, the arresting officer mistook his plain coat for the garb of a priest and did not give him a ticket. The conversation usually went something like this: "Oh, I'm sorry, Father! You were just exceeding the speed limit out here and I know you wouldn't want to hurt anyone." "Thank you." To which John added, "I not always, but frequently, put a religious book or Bible or Testament on the dash going through customs, for immigration to Canada and back. It would say as much as I could tell them, perhaps—in shorter compass." The effectiveness of the Bible on prominent display in the car is illustrated by this account:

> My father was a minister ordained by lot . . . [and wore] the plain coat. It happened that he was a salesman and would have his Bible along. And one time his Bible was on the seat and . . . I think he was parked too close to a fire hydrant or sticking out over a parking lot. And when he left, the traffic policeman there stopped him and then said, "Father, I would have given you a ticket, but I saw the Bible in your seat."

Two other stories show how Mennonite ministers deliberately exploited their plain coats to receive favors from the government:

> This is a true story. When Levi Hartzler [1909-2002] and Nelson Litwiller [1898-1986] went to Mennonite World Conference, they came back together. They had to go through customs. And all the time they were [in Europe] they didn't wear their plain coats. And when they got off the plane, Lit was smart. He put his plain coat on. And so they went through customs. Levi was in line. And they saw Lit and they called him out, and they passed him through customs—just like that. When Lit passed Levi, he waved at him. He said, "Goodbye!" And there was Levi, laughing. He said, "Boy, leave it to him!"

John Mosemann told a different version of what was probably the same event, although more through the eyes of Nelson Litwiller than Levi Hartzler:

> It was one of the Mennonite world conferences—presumably in the 50s or early 60s. They still traveled by boat. A number of these persons who had attended the conference had quite a discussion . . . on the value and relevance of the clerical coat. None of them were really over-enthused about its value or its place and usefulness, Litwiller among them. He was not making a case for this at all—until they docked at New York. That morning he put on his clerical vest and he picked out an Irish official, went up to him and said, "Do I have to stand in all this line to get through customs and immigration?" "No, Father, you just follow me." And so he took Litwiller on one side of the barricade, which was pierced. You could see through it. And the other representatives, travelers, who he had discussed this issue with, were on the other side, waiting their turns. And he waved to them as he passed by. And it took them an hour

or two to get through. . . . He demonstrated that the clerical vest had some time-saving value. He let the cloth speak for itself.

Here Litwiller was wearing a clerical vest with a lapel coat. But if he "let the cloth speak for itself," he also became an aggressive trickster by deliberately wearing the coat for a non-clerical purpose and by deliberately seeking out an Irish official, who would be by nature inclined to give favors to a presumed Catholic priest.

John Mosemann relished telling another story about J. C. Wenger wearing a plain coat and allowing himself to be mistaken for a Catholic priest—but this time by a fellow Mennonite—Ed Taylor (1923-2006), an African-American employed at the time by the Mennonite Board of Missions and Charities:

> Ed Taylor had determined that he was going to witness to any priests that got on [the train] at South Bend. Ed Taylor had a certain book, and this priest that came and sat next to him showed interest in this book—it was one of John R. Stott's books—and asked him whether he reads much by Stott. Yes, everything he can get his hands on of Stott's. They were visiting and he finally asked Ed what he does. Well, he works for the Mennonite Board of Missions. He's their Home Missions secretary, and so on and so on and so on. "And what's your name?" "Ed Taylor." And Ed Taylor reciprocated and wanted to know who he was. He said, "I'm J. C. Wenger."

Wenger clearly relishes being mistaken for a Catholic priest. He prolongs the conversation during the mistaken identity and does not reveal his name until the protocol of conversation makes it absolutely necessary. Or, at least that's the case in Mosemann's personal shaping of the story in the manner of the Mennonite legend of the plain coat preacher.

Although such stories are almost always told about Mennonite men tricksters, one shows the similar possibility latent in the "cape" dresses worn by conservative Mennonite women:

> This actually happened. Mary Ann Bender [1904-2001?] and Uriah Bontrager's wife [Esther Irene Bender 1918-84] went to California to visit John Bender [b. 1899?] .... Anyway, John was taking them sight-seeing and they went into a park somewhere. A man looks into the back seat and he says, "Oh, sisters! [Catholic nuns]." Uriah [1907-74] piped up right away, "No, sisters-in-law."

Even if some of these stories are based on incidents in real life, the reader can clearly perceive that they all fit within the archetypal narrative of the plain-coat preacher in mistaken communication with the world. The shaping of such narratives into stylized form is best captured by the following version, whose punch lines are Bible verses not likely ever to have been used in a conversation between policeman and Mennonite:

> There was a preacher coming from Ohio and he was going too fast. So he got stopped—pulled over by a cop. The cop walked up to him and the preacher looked back to the cop and he says, "Be merciful to me, a sinner!" And the cop shook his hand and he says, "Go thy way, and sin no more!" That's all he said. And he left.

That version, told by a Conservative Mennonite man, assumes—but does not mention—that the plain coat resembles a priest's. Perhaps it and others also participate in a larger cycle of legends told by

More Trickster Tales

members of other religious groups about their clergy. Here is a Methodist variant as told by a Mennonite missionary doctor who worked with Methodists in India:

> [Dr. Miller, a Methodist in Nepal] said the Methodist Church tells about this itinerant preacher who was out gathering money for the churches. He got on the stagecoach to go home. And a robber got on the stagecoach and started to go around, person to person: "Give me your money. Give me your money. Give me your money." He came to this Methodist preacher and [the preacher] said, "Oh, please, please, please! I'm just a poor Methodist preacher. I've got church money here." [The robber said] "Oh, you're a Methodist? So am I, Father. So am I. So you just keep it. Keep it."

There is a bit of story contamination here, since the Methodist robber would never have addressed his fellow Methodist clergyman as "Father." That part of the narrative belongs in a trickster story where the would-be victim is mistaken for a Catholic priest. The story no doubt assumes that the Methodist clergyman was wearing his clergyman's garb.

Tricky Redemption

Mennonites sometimes express concern about telling such stories—especially repeating the story of Menno in the stagecoach—lest it convey to the younger generation the notion that deception, whether by design or by default, is excusable in Christian affairs. J. C. Wenger told one story and then overtly defended its subtext.

> Well, I heard Peter Dyck [1914-2010] tell that he was helping a Mennonite boy—I think around twelve—to escape from Russia into the free world [following World War 2].

And the boy was scared stiff, of course. And Peter said, "Don't you say anything. Let me do the talking." So when they got to the border, Peter showed the Russian that had to leave them out his own papers, which were in order. And then he showed a driver's license, which was supposedly the passport for this boy. And the Russian couldn't read any other language, so he let them go through. So Peter Dyck got that boy out on a driver's license. I assume it was his own. But he just flashed the card in front of the Russian and he said, "OK?" And the Russian said, "OK." No, he didn't lie. You get to the point, when you live under the Russians, that you're pretty slippery. I'm not justifying it—the battle of wits—[but it shows] how to get along.

J. C. Wenger may not be "justifying it" logically, but he is justifying it by telling a moving story. He might have thought of citing the ambiguous admonition by Jesus: "Be wise as serpents and innocent as doves." Or he might have told this final story, which illustrates that the "Mennonite Lie" might not be necessary—that, in fact, a blatant telling of the literal truth might also disarm would-be oppressors:

A Mennonite brother in an elevator with one companion was asked to hand over his wallet. He said he didn't have his wallet with him that day. While [the robber] pondered his next threat, the brother added, "But I have $20 in my shirt pocket." The would-be assailant made no further demand but got out of the elevator at the first opportunity.

· FOUR ·

Amish Slurs

MENNONITES HAVE an ambivalent attitude toward the Amish, who are the near relatives of Swiss-Alsatian Mennonites through shared history, ethnicity and religious values. On the one hand, Mennonites admire the way the Amish remain steadfast to many Anabaptist principles that Mennonites themselves have compromised over the past decades. On the other hand, Mennonites want to separate themselves from these "backward" people with whom they are too often confused by the rest of the world In that ambivalence, Mennonites resemble American culture at large, as interpreted by David Weaver-Zercher in his book *The Amish in the American Imagination* (Johns Hopkins 2001), which shows how Americans at times idealize the Amish for preserving traditional values and at other times ridicule them for their cultural lag.

The result of this ambivalence is that Mennonites sometimes tell stories that ridicule the Amish and sometimes tell stories that defend, or idealize them. This first chapter of Amish stories will consist of stories that satirize the Amish, and the following chapter will present stories that defend the Amish. The two chapters were combined in "Amish Joking," published in the July 15, 2009, issue of the online *Journal of Mennonite Writing*.

Old Tales

Three old stories from Pennsylvania-German culture persist so much in storytelling about the Amish today that they will be used to open this chapter. They establish the point that many humorous stories about the Amish are survivals that have been inherited by the Amish as the last obvious representatives of that German-American immigrant culture. The first story depicts a surprisingly noncommittal church leader:

> The deacon was supposed to deal with church conflicts, at least at the early stages, and they were having problems in their church. And the one party came to the deacon's house and gave their side of the story. And he said, "Ja, ja, ja. Du est recht [You have a point. You are right.]." And then they left. After a while the other side—their people—came and they told him their side of the story. And his response was the same: "Ja, ja, ja. Du est recht." And his wife had been around all this time, of course, and after the second one left," Why" she said, "John, you talk the same to both sides. They both came. They gave you their side of the story, and you kept telling each side that they were right. They can't both be right." He said, "Ja, Mommy. Du est a recht! [You are right, too!]."

The other two stories show Amish husbands and wives in more overt conflict:

> This was told at Little Eden Camp [Onekema, Michigan] in front of the snack shop. It was told by Jesse Short [1894-1962]—a bishop [from Archbold, Ohio] and he got it from Roy Otto [1902-1992], a bishop from Springs, Pennsylvania. They all understood Pennsylvania Dutch so it made it more realistic. . . . This happened in Pennsylvania. This

Amish lady's husband was very sick. And so she went over to the neighbors to call the doctor. The doctor in this rural community could also speak Pennsylvania Dutch. And he came to the house, to the door, and knocked. She went to the door and she said: "Come on, Doctor. Doctor, John is aller krank. He's very sick." He came in, looked him over. And they had him propped up on an easy chair and he didn't look very well to the doctor. He went over, took his pulse. He said, "What! John ist todt! John is dead!" And his wife said, "John!" But John wasn't dead. And so John said, "Ich bin nicht todt." And his wife said, "John, sie stille! Be quiet, John. The doctor knows more than you do!"

An Amish bridegroom was driving his new bride away from the wedding ceremony in the horsedrawn buggy. When the horse began to act up, he lashed it with the whip severely. "That's one!" he said. His new wife protested mildly his harsh treatment of the horse. Farther down the road, the horse acted up again. He whipped it even harder. "That's two!" he said. His wife protested again. Farther down the road, the horse really acted up. The Amishman got out his pistol and shot the horse dead. "That's three!" he said. Then his wife soundly berated him for his cruelty and brutality. She really jawed him out. Turning to her, he said, "That's one!"

This story is a Mennonite version of the very common tale type known by folktale specialists as "The Taming of the Shrew." Amish society is overtly patriarchal, especially in that women are given no public leadership roles in the church. But the patriarchy is more respectful of woman than is shown in that brutal story, and Amish women tend to be very self-directed in domestic matters.

Patriarchy is more gently satirized in the following story, where the humor depends on the Amish woman pronouncing "Christ" not as in "Jesus Christ" but as in the man's name "Chris," short for "Christian."

> This Amish woman walked into the bookstore and she saw this motto on the wall there: "Christ Is the Head of This House." She walked up to the cashier and asked, very cautiously: "Do you have any sign like that that says, 'Jake Is the Head of This House'?"

Peculiar Customs

Most Amish stories make fun of the many ways in which they reject mainstream material culture and go their own way in regard to costume, transportation and modern technology. Two stories are based on the fact that adult male members of the church are expected to let their beards grow untrimmed. (However, they shave off their mustaches, presumably because mustaches were required in Napoleon's army.)

> An Amishman had such a long, flowing beard. And someone who was not Amish asked him, "When you sleep at night, do you put the beard under the covers or on top of the covers?" It never occurred to him to think about that before! So that night when he went to bed, he put his beard under the covers, and it didn't seem right. And out of the covers, and it didn't seem right. And this went on all night and the poor man got no sleep.

> Did you hear about the Amish lady that was having such a dream! Sort of a funny one, or difficult one. She was having breakfast and eating shredded wheat. She had an awful time getting rid of this shredded wheat. And

finally she woke up and here she was chewing on her husband's beard!

Although the Amish today tend to build their own new houses, in a distinctive style, earlier they more frequently bought pre-existing houses and altered them to fit their peculiar needs. In such situations, electric wiring had to be removed.

An electrician in the Fort Wayne-Grabill [Indiana] area was asked by an Amishman to come and unhook the electricity at a house that he had purchased in the Grabill area. The electrician said he would be there to do what is necessary. "But," he said, "you're going to have to call the I and M [Indiana and Michigan utilities company] and tell them to unhook the juice. . . . So the Amishman went next door and he called the power company and said, "I bought a property," and he named where it was, and he said, "Come and unhook the juice." And the company said, "Sure, we'll be there, such and such a time." The day arrived. They didn't come. So the Amishman went back to the neighbor, called the company again, and said, "I asked you one time to come and unhook the juice." "Sure, we'll be there." The time came. The power company didn't appear and the Amishman was quite upset. He called them a third time and said, "I asked you to come and unhook the power and you haven't done it, so," he said, "I'm going to go and take all the light bulbs out and let the juice run out!"

Although the Amish still do not use electricity in their homes, the technological ignorance of that Amish man is belied today by Amish workers in home construction and manufactured housing plants who are expert electricians.

Using horse and buggy for transportation instead of automobiles is probably the most striking Amish characteristic in their public image for Americans. Four stories derive from Amish horse culture. The first refers to recent state government regulations saying that their buggies need to bear bright red reflective warning signs on the back side. Some conservative Amish groups vigorously resisted the requirement as being too flashy, too attention-getting, hence too prideful. But most Amish have accepted red reflectors.

> My sister in the Middlebury area actually heard an Amish lady bemoaning the fact that they had to paint the sign on the back of their buggy bright red. If they could only paint it black, it would be so much nicer!

The second story uses the horse to comment on the difficulty of attaining the Amish goal of *gelassenheit,* meaning yieldedness, or humility.

> One Amishman found himself feeling too proud of the fine horse he owned. So he sold it and bought an old nag instead. Then he found himself being proud of his humility.

The story recalls one on the similar problem of humility in Mennonite culture that uses clothing rather than horses as a measure of humility: Driving home after church, the Mennonite man turned to his wife and said, "I think we were the plainest that was there today."

> A man bought a horse from an Amishman, assuming that the integrity of the Amish faith guaranteed a high quality horse. Upon receiving and inspecting the horse, he found that it was an inferior animal. So he went back to the Amishman and asked if he could borrow his plain-cut coat.

"Why?" asked the Amishman. "Because I want to sell a horse," the man replied.

Over at Shipshewana [Indiana] there was an Amishman who was a prominent man in the church. Someone asked him whether he thought the time would come when the Amish would have cars. And he said, "Yeah," he thinks the time will come. But he's afraid it won't come quick enough for him!

More Peculiarities

Like "Yoder" in Mennonite culture, "Stoltzfus" is one of the most typical Amish family names in Lancaster County, Pennsylvania.

Have you heard of the Stoltzfus Factory? These people went to Pennsylvania for the first time and they went around, were driving down the road there, and there was just Stoltzfus on the mailbox. They went around the next corner, and there's another Stoltzfus! Turned the other corner, and there's a Stoltzfus! Turned another corner and there's a Stoltzfus! And finally they turned another corner and then they saw why: There was a "Stoltzfus Factory."

The manufacture of house trailers, recreational vehicles and manufactured housing is a major part of the economy in north-central Indiana, site of the nation's third-largest Amish community. Many Amish men now work in such factories. A common saying is that Goshen (or Wakarusa or Middlebury or Nappanee) is the only place in the world where you can jaywalk across a downtown street and be hit by a house. The following story imagines an even larger house on the road:

A couple of years ago out east of town here, there was an Amish family that got a house trailer—a double-wide. And they put a basement under it. Someone was talking about this—that these people got a house trailer with a basement under it. And this one woman said that she wishes she could see that thing go down the road with a basement under it!

Additional joking stories about the Amish appear in the dialect stories of Chapter 6 and the bawdy stories of Chapter 7.

· FIVE ·

The Amish Joke Back

IDEALLY, IN A CHAPTER devoted to stories that show Amish people in a positive light, or gaining the upper hand in a debate, all of the examples should come from the Amish themselves in order to show how they define themselves, positively, through traditional narratives. Unfortunately, that is not the case. As I mentioned before, that would require recording their stories as told in their native language, Pennsylvania German. Although I have Amish friends, I do not speak their German dialect. Consequently, I cannot "pick up" stories from natural conversational flow and it would be awkward, if not impossible, to arrange for story-telling sessions with Amish narrators, around a tape-recorder.

Most of the stories in this chapter come from the same Mennonite informants whose stories satirizing the Amish appear in the preceding chapter—which suggests that Mennonites identify themselves with Amish as often as they dissociate themselves from them.

The stories here that probably come closest to revealing Amish self-perceptions are taken from the published writings of William R. McGrath (1931-2015), who converted to the Beachy Amish (Amish-Mennonite) faith and for many years was a leader of that denomination. He became an ordained minister in 1956 and attracted a following of Beachy and Old Order Amish who were interested in missions and herbal medicine. Eventually he led a colony of believers to Costa Rica and later became a missionary to Ireland, where he died.

His defense of the Amish community (including himself) resulted in a number of pithy stories included in his book, *Amish Folk Remedies for Plain and Fancy Ailments* (Minerva, Ohio, 1984), which appealed to Amish readers. The source is duly recognized below. Several stories are also reprinted from Elmer L. Smith's *Pennsylvania Dutch Folklore* (1960), which includes non-Amish variants of some of the stories that McGrath offers as Amish narratives. The other stories come from oral performances that I tape-recorded.

The Smart Dutchman

As a man with a college education, McGrath was well aware that the Amish today suffer from the old American stereotype of being the "Dumb Dutchman." He explicitly recognized the association in two brief accounts. In the second one, he accepts the Amish as fitting into the generic category of "Dutch" but illustrates the smartness of a Dutch—here probably meaning Amish—waitress. In the first story, dumbness is not denied, but smartness is found in the Amish boy's witty response. Both show that the Dutch, including the Amish, are smarter than their critics. Indeed, in almost all of the stories borrowed from McGrath below, smart, witty retorts create the appeal of the pithy narratives.

> Dumb Dutch? Many stories are told about the supposedly "dumb Dutch." What appears to the public to be "dumb" may often be a kind of a shrewd peasant logic. An Amish proverb says, "We get too soon old and too late smart." An Amish boy tried to explain the backwardness of his brother to the teacher by saying, "It ain't he can't learn, it's just he doesn't remember anything he learns." A tourist complained about the chicken being tough in a Dutch

restaurant and the Dutch waitress replied: "It's tougher when there's none." (McGrath 73)

The story that circulates most widely in Mennonite circles and defends the Amish against dumbness is the following:

> A New York tourist was traveling west on Route 340 near Intercourse, Pennsylvania, when he noticed an elderly Amishman pumping water just in front of his barn. He stopped his car and called to the Amishman, "Could you tell me how to get to route 30?" The Amishman pretended he didn't hear and kept on pumping water. Again the tourist called louder, "I'm lost. Could you please tell me how to get to Route 30?" The Amishman kept on pumping. Rather angrily the tourist yelled, "I knew you Amish were dumb, but I didn't know you were so dumb." The Amishman stopped pumping and replied, "I may be dumb, but at least I ain't lost."

The narrator thinks "this rather humorous incident took place near Intercourse, Pennsylvania, several years ago." However, the wide, generic circulation of the tale shows that it is a traditional story, and probably even one told long ago about Pennsylvania Dutch people in general and more recently localized with the Amish. Does the Amish reply about his not being "lost" also have spiritual implications?

The Amish and Other Groups

In *Pennsylvania Dutch Folklore* Elmer L. Smith included two stories that compare the Amish to other religious groups. The first story probably vindicates the Amish as a practical, rural people, even though it implicitly criticizes them for lacking the spiritual and moral values of the other two groups. The second story also seems to vindicate the conservative Amishman, whose "motion" supersedes and cancels out all of the previous three:

> A story is told that reflects the interest an Amishman takes in his herd, and at the same time the shrewdness of the Amish as compared to other farmers. A Quaker, a Hutterite and an Amish farmer were given two cows each. The Quaker gave one of his cows to a less fortunate neighbor; the Hutterite turned his two cows over to the elders of his communal group, who in turn gave him some of the milk; while the Amishman kept one cow and traded the other one for a bull. (Smith 19)

> The Amish people favor the maintenance of the small country school with all its traditions of the past. Most communities have abandoned the one-room school in favor of consolidated schools. The story is told of a meeting of a local school board in Lancaster County, at which time discussion was centered on building a new school to replace the old one-room school. The board was composed of an Amishman, a Methodist, a Catholic and a Presbyterian. The following motions were made [and passed?] in successive order: Catholic: "I move we build a new school house." Methodist: "I make a second move that we build the new school on the same ground where the old school is." Presbyterian: "I make a third move that we use the material from the present school to help build the new one." Amishman: "I make a fourth move that we stay right in the old school house until the new one is completed." (Smith 19)

The logic of the stories requires that, for the nonce, we disregard the fact that the Amish and the Hutterites have never settled close to each other and that an Amishman is not likely to serve on a public school board.

Defending Peculiar Customs

A number of stories replicate the encounter of the tourist-outsider with Amish people and show the Amish defending their odd practices with witty retorts:

> One Amishman was pointed at by an obese tourist lady who said: "Look at the odd man!" Returning her look, he saw her paint, powder, artificial hairstyle, gaudy clothes and bulging shorts, and could not resist replying: "It wonders me who is really the ODD ONE!" (McGrath 71-72)

> Another tourist is reported to have said to an Amishman, "I once grew a beard like yours, but when I saw how terrible I looked, I shaved it off!" The Amishman coolly replied: "I used to have a face like yours, too, and when I saw how terrible it looked, I grew a beard." (McGrath 72; Smith 19)

> The Amish are curious about television, rock music, radios and the drug culture, but they avoid all these things because they see the results are crime, juvenile delinquency, divorce, nervous breakdowns and social disorders. An Amishman was asked if he did not miss radio and television. He replied, "They are selling something I don't need: entertainment, multiplying your wants for things you don't need, and discontentment. It is not so much what you eat that makes you sick, but what is eating you because of what you are looking at and listening to. I don't envy you, I pity you."(McGrath 75)

Notice the blunt, aggressive put-downs that create the rather dark humor in these stories. Does that characterize the Amish sense of humor? Or is it a manifestation of McGrath, the preacher-prophet who is reporting the stories? The latter possibility is found in a final story from McGrath that ends in a lesson from the Bible instead:

> While some Amish are gullible, as in any group of people, most are quite shrewd enough not to panic like many of their English neighbors. Watching a parade of protestors against nuclear war, an Amishman was asked, "Aren't you afraid of the Third World War?" He replied, "The Bible says there will be wars and rumors of wars until the End, then Jesus will come. Only a fool would fear the wars and not fear God Who will judge all mankind." (McGrath 74)

Outsiders may not find humor here, but the Amish might, especially since the story characterizes the enquirer as a "fool," as do the more humorous stories that precede it. The possibility that blunt put-downs are relished by the Amish comes from a story told by a non-Amish informant about an incident he claimed to have observed. The fact that the put-down is not clearly relevant to the conversation that leads up to it suggests an interest in put-downs *per se*. But the woman's retort may equally be a vindication that the Amish indeed do not and should not "see things alike" other groups.

> There was an Amish woman among the men and women waiting in a doctor's office in Nappanee [Indiana]. And one of the non-Amish men was discussing denominations and said, "Why can't they get together? Why can't they all see things alike?" And then another gentleman said, "If they did, you would never have gotten a wife." And [the first man] said, "I would have gotten her all right." And then

the stately Amish grandma said, "If all the people would see alike, no one would have wanted you."

A story from real life shows a young Amish woman using the put down in a—to Mennonites—humorous way. It was told to me by the Mennonite man who wore the shorts:

> A young Amishman by the name of Wenger was doing his [alternate to military] alternate] service at the [Mennonite Biblical] seminary here [then at Goshen College, Indiana] as custodian. His wife came to work at our house. But as is so often the case, I had to go pick her up out in the country where they lived. This one summer day I was wearing shorts—Bermuda shorts. Nevertheless, when we finally did get to Eighth Street, she asked me, "You're Mennonite, aren't you?" I said, "Yeah. Why did you ask?" "Well, because of those shorts that you're wearing. Is that really modest?" I said, "Oh, well, I'm just wearing those because it's so insufferably hot." "Well," she said, there are some places where it's a lot hotter!"

Other kinder, gentler stories told about Amish by Mennonites also defend, in their own way, Amish practices:

> An Italian visitor, who grew weary of the long, drawn-out [Amish wedding] ceremony, said, "It takes you too long to tie the knot." To which his Amish friend replied, "But have you ever seen one of our knots come loose?" — John Ruth

> Big Perry B. Miller from Topeka—he's dead and gone now; gone to his reward—was an Amishman that always had a lot of fun. He was a quick wit. He had a Beachy

Amish man, who had a beard and a black hat, with a van, take a whole load [of Amish] out west. At the one place where they stopped for gas, the attendant at the gas station was pumping gas and Big Perry B. was standing there and [the attendant] looked in the van, stroked his chin a little and says, "Indiana!" And Perry says, "Yes." [The attendant] says, "Does everybody in Indiana have beards?" And Big Perry paused a little and he said, "No. The women don't."

An Amishman was brought before the judge and the court to testify as to the kind of car that was involved in a certain kind of accident. [The Amishman] was scratching his head and trying to remember whether it was a Pontiac or a Buick. The judge says, "Can't you tell the difference between these kinds of cars?" And [the Amishman] turned around and said to him, "No," he says. "Can you tell the difference between the different kinds of buggies you see on the road?"

The dumb outsider who gawks uncomprehendingly at Amish people is put in his place by one story:

A tourist from New York came to Lancaster County to look for the Amish. And he was frantically searching for them all over. So finally he asked one of the people, who happened to be a Mennonite. The Mennonite was rather protective of the Amish and also had a good sense of humor. He says, "Oh, you won't find any of the Amish now. It's their mating season."

The following story possibly derives from some Mennonites' insistence that you can tell an Amishman by his posture—bent slightly forward, walking in a rather lumbering gait, arms akimbo or clasping hands behind his back—which implies his rural background and hard work as a farmer. Here an Amishman embraces that identity in a self-deprecating way:

> A family of Amishmen, visiting the Pittsburgh Zoo, were standing in front of the monkey and apes display [demonstrates posture: feet spread apart, arms hanging freely]. When they turned around, they discovered many people grouped behind them, staring at them. So the Amish father walked away, imitating the walk, posture, and movements of an ape, saying: "We just escaped from the cage."

Story for Story Sake

Even William McGrath, preacher and prophet, appreciated an "Amish" story for its own sake, as shown by the two that follow. Notice, however, that the first one invokes a Bible verse for its justification.

> Because the Bible says, "A merry heart doeth good like a medicine," the Amish appreciate humor. One Amishman replied to a man who splashed mortar on him and asked if he was hurt. "No, I'm just mortified!" (McGrath 72; Smith 21)

> A group of school boys tried to scare little Amos, an Amish boy. They jumped out at him with an imitation skeleton. He didn't bat an eyelash so they asked, "Aren't you afraid of spooks and skeletons?" Amos replied, "Why, there ain't no such thing as a ghost, and a skeleton is nothing but a stack of bones with the people scraped off." (McGrath 74; Smith 26)

One story comes from an ex-Amish informant from the Amish community in Lancaster, Pennsylvania, and shows an Amish trickster vindicated in a conversation with his own minister:

> The Amishman had flown to Israel. One Sunday morning he and his wife were asked to sit in front of the congregation. They were subjected to "counsel." The minister asked if it was true that they had flown to Israel—[flying in an airplane] is against the rules. "No," the Amishman said. He did not fly the plane. The pilot did. He was absolved of guilt.

Amish Values in Stories

Beyond the peculiar rules of conduct, two stories communicate some of the deeper values found in Amish culture. On the surface, the first one makes fun of the Amish work ethic, although it also implies awe in regard to their commitment to hard work. The second one, told by a young Mennonite man, affirms the redemptive effect of Amish pacifism and nonviolence:

> It was reported that during World War II the government, which was rationing gasoline and shoes, wanted to put the Amish on an eight-hour day. They replied, "That's interesting. But what would we do after dinner?"

> I've heard a story for a long time about a group of boys, probably from the Mennonite church, who wanted to play a trick on an Amishman. And so they took his buggy apart on Halloween night and reassembled it on the roof of his barn. And the Amishman woke up in the middle of the night and saw all this going on. And so he told his wife to get up and prepare a big meal. About daybreak these guys

were coming off the roof of the barn and he was down there waiting on them. And he invited them in for breakfast, since they had been working so hard. And they went in and had this big breakfast and they felt so bad they went back out and disassembled it.

The student who told me this story told me he read it in *Coals of Fire*, a Mennonite inspirational book of stories by Elizabeth Bauman (Scottdale, PA: Herald Press, 1954).

Not really. But in Chapter 8, "The Mystery of the Thatch," he might have read a European Mennonite variant on which it is based. Bauman tells the story of "Preacher Peter" in the Emmental of Switzerland who, with his wife, woke up one night to the sound of men removing the thatch from the roof of their house. Peter asked his wife to prepare a meal, to which he invited the thieves. Instead of eating, they replaced the thatch and left.

Although Bauman says that "the chief incidents in each story are true," (v) she actually borrowed the story from John Horsch's book, *The Principles of Nonresistance as Held by the Mennonites* (Scottdale, PA: Mennonite Publishing House, 1939), and Horsch's telling of it is based, in turn, on a variant found in J. Ellenberger's *Bilder aus dem Pilgerleben: Gesammelt in der Mennoniten-Gemeinde*, 3 vols (Frankfurt A.M., 1880). Although the Library of Congress regards Ellenberger's book as "fiction," the thatch/buggy story is actually a legend (see Chapters 8-10), or a story believed to be true, that becomes altered according to the place and time of its telling. In this case, the Swiss preacher and his house become the Indiana Amishman and his buggy. In all cases, this humble story helps the Anabaptist community preserve one of its most cherished values, as embodied by the note Bauman attaches to her chapter: "Do good to them that hate you." (Mt. 5:44)

In the contemporary variant, the Mennonite community revises one of its old stories into a story about the Amish in order to preserve traditional Mennonite values. Attributing to the Amish what was once Mennonite might reflect Mennonites' implicit awareness of the slippage of traditional values in Mennonite communities but their better preservation in Amish culture.

· SIX ·

Dialect Stories

THE ALSATIAN GERMAN dialect that developed in the United States as Pennsylvania-Dutch/German remains the native language of Old Order Amish groups in the U.S. and Canada. Children learn to speak it as their first language and it remains the language spoken at home, although a version of High, or Standard, German is used in Amish church services and English is used in public discourse and writing. It is also the native language of Old Order Mennonites, although other Mennonites gave up German for English, beginning around the time of World War 1. Mennonites may have a few verses of German printed in their hymnals, and they may retain German words, phrases and inflections in their speech, but nowadays their use of Spanish probably rivals their mastery of German.

The continued use of German by the Amish makes them one of the last—and certainly the most recognizable—"German" groups in the U.S. and Canada. Hence, the Amish tend to become the brunt of most or all of the old dialect stories that make fun of people who speak German rather than standard English. Mennonites may remember a few such stories from their own background, but the dialect stories they tell most often make the Amish the brunt of the joke. In telling such jokes, acculturated Mennonites can separate themselves from their own "backward" past, as well as from the Amish, who are a visual reminder of that past and whom outsiders too often confuse with Mennonites—to the Mennonites' chagrin.

Puns

The humor of many dialect jokes comes from a word or phrase spoken in one language being misunderstood for the hilarious meaning of the same sounds in the receiver's native language.

> Some city folks from Chicago or New York came to Goshen [Indiana] to look at some Amish. When they saw some walk down the street, they tailed them closely, hoping to overhear them talking Pennsylvania Dutch. The Amish were quiet for quite some time, until finally one of them said to the other, "Was sachs du?" To which the city-slicker responded, "I think they lost."

In Pennsylvania Dutch *Was sachs du?* means "What do you know?" Of course, the city folks think the Amish are talking about the Red Sox or White Sox baseball team. Here the English city-slickers are ridiculed, not the dialect-speaking Amish.

The punch line of the following story depends on knowing that *hira* (pronounced hire-a) means *marry* in Pennsylvania Dutch:

> A man once came to an Amish family . . . and they had a family of girls. The mother was on the porch sweeping. He comes up and says that he has a family of children. He needs to be away and he needs to hire a babysitter. Could he hire one of her daughters? "Which one would you want?" "Oh, it doesn't matter. Any one of them will do." And then she took after him very angrily with the broom. — J. C. Wenger

The unlikelihood of an Amish woman even considering a proposal of marriage by an English man suggests that this story is one that has migrated to the Amish from an earlier Pennsylvania German culture.

One Amish story is based on the pronunciation of English *v* as *w* in German.

> There was an Amish man who didn't have any luck with his wives. He was married three times. Each time his wife died. He was at the funeral of his third wife—at the viewing—and all of a sudden he fainted. The preacher leading the funeral saw that he had fainted, and said, "Don't worry, folks. He will re-wive."

Two final stories based on puns are located in particular Mennonite communities—Wauseon in northwestern Ohio and Spring House in eastern Pennsylvania—although originally they might have been attributed to non-Mennonite speakers of German from the same areas:

> An Amishman went for a ride in Ohio, on this train ride. Obviously it was something new for him and the conductor kept coming through the passenger cars, announcing the next station. "Wau-see-on! Wau-see-on! Wau-see-on!" He said this about three times in the car where the Amishman was riding. And he said, "Conductor, he <u>was</u> on but he got off at Toledo."

> There's a little town outside of Philadelphia called Spring House. The story is told of the conductor of Reading Railroad who, as he was from Souderton, had a Dutchified accent. Some Mennonites were on the train that day and

> the conductor called out, "Shpring Rouse!" And all the Mennonites jumped out.

German *spring rous* means "jump out."

Mistaken Words and Idioms

Even more stories are based on failure to learn idiomatic English. Often the humor comes from translating German literally into English, sometimes in regard to single words but more often in regard to idiomatic phrase structure.

> There are more Southeastern Iowa stories. The [telephone] party line was really going—a man who lost his third or fourth wife. On the party line they were saying, "Joe Miller's wife died again."

> A student at Goshen College became a doctor and took up practice at Orrville, Ohio, and there are a good many Amish in that community. He discovered, after a time, that they were asking him to make house calls simply because they knew it didn't take him very long to drive out, but it took them a long time to drive horse and buggy in. This became rather disgusting to him, and he decided the next time somebody tries to get him to make a house call, he'll find out if it's really necessary. So in due time a woman called up and she said: "My man, he is sick. Could you come out?" And he kind of snapped at her. He said, "Is he bedfast?" Well, she didn't know that word. And she said, "No, he's just laying there—loose-like." — J. C. Wenger.

> The people at the bank in Kalona [Iowa] got such a bang out of a check they saw. There was a Conservative [Mennonite]

or an Amish man that was ill, and they hired a nurse to work for them. So when he wrote out a check to her, down below he wanted to write what the check was for—where it says "For?" And so he wrote, "Sick in bed—with nurse."

When he first was teaching, probably in a one-room schoolhouse, . . . he had some students come in who were just learning to speak English. It was an Amish boy, or Old Order Mennonite. I don't know. It was raining heavily one day and it was doing some flooding and there was some water across the road. This little boy said, "Oh, look, the water's walking across the road."

Language Transition

Two stories involve church leaders confused by language during a time of transition from German to English:

A [Mennonite] minister in Pennsylvania heard some young people express a desire for someone to preach in English. He said he could, and proceeded to do so. At one point he referred to girls with horz hair and pointed to the new convicts sitting in the front of the church. — John Ruth

My grandmother Hannah Clemens [1880-1977] told me about one of the song leaders at Souderton [Pennsylvania] Mennonite Church that she remembered from long ago. He would announce the number [of the hymn] 222: "Now, let's sing two-tooty-two."

One story depicts the plight of an Amish preacher who may use English in everyday affairs but gets confused due to the pressure of being in the public eye during the Sunday sermon, when he is supposed to be using Standard German, which he has not mastered.

> There's a story told about an Amish preacher who got so much English in. He was telling about what a brave man [the prophet] Daniel was and he said, "Und de lions and de Daniel warh net geharmed whatsoever."

The story was told by J. C. Wenger, who imitated Amish folk preaching style by adding a chanted, sing-song quality to the direct quotation.

Ethnics sometimes conceal their ethnicity when it is disfavored and, at other times, flaunt it when they can benefit from it. So, too, with language and dialect.

> Abe Moyer [of Souderton, Pennsylvania 1873-1952?] was driving a car with a number of brethren in it and a policeman stopped him. I forgot what he made—some minor blooper of some sort. And the policeman bawled him out. And Abe pretended he couldn't understand English. He turned to the other people in the car and he said, "Was secht der mann? [What's the guy saying?]" Finally, the policeman said, "Get out of here, you dumb Dutchman."
> — J. C. Wenger

Finally, a story, told about a generic Pennsylvania German who tried hard to be English, illustrates that one cannot ever forget one's native language, no matter how hard one may try.

> A young man grew up in that [Pennsylvania German] community and, of course, German was his mother tongue. He was gone from the community for three years and he came

back and said, "I don't understand anything any more. I've forgotten it all completely. I'm now completely English." But he said one evening he walked across the lawn, and it was dusk and somebody had left a rake lie with the teeth up. He stepped on the teeth and the handle came up and hit him on the head. He said he not only knew the Dutch word for rake, he knew how to describe it! — J. C. Wenger

In the history of human speech, the words that remain the most stable over time are those used intimately in homes. They include words for family relationships, everyday tasks—and obscenities and profanities.

· SEVEN ·

Bawdy Tales

YES, MENNONITES being human, are also fascinated by taboo subjects—whether profane, obscene or merely vulgar. Chapter 1 presented a number of bawdy riddle-jokes, including the very popular ones about "two men a night" and intercourse standing up, and a few shady tales also appear in other chapters. I am surprised that there are not more such stories in my collection.

Of course, I was not expecting audiences of Mennonites to contribute bawdy stories in public settings. In fact, on occasion I was corrected by audience members, following the program, for telling a story that was too naughty for the setting. The stories in this chapter were usually told in one-on-one conversations or in small groups of closely-knit friends and relatives, where it is "safe" to tell such stories in Mennonite culture.

Printing them here might also be a bit risky—somewhat like telling them in public to a Mennonite audience. Their proper venue is informal and intimate situations, not public discourse. Knowing that Katie Funk Wiebe was roundly criticized for publishing stories using the word "Hell" in her folk humor column in *Festival Quarterly*, which is not even a church-sponsored publication, I can also expect criticism for including them here. But any survey of a group's storytelling tradition must include a report and assessment of how they handle taboo content in folk narratives. I will invoke my literary hero

79

Geoffrey Chaucer (c.1343-1400), author of *The Canterbury Tales*, and interpret the chapter by saying that to omit, improve or censor such things would be to falsify reality, which is also immoral. In Chaucer studies it's called the Doctrine of Moral Realism.

It should not be necessary to make a defense of the bawdy Mennonite tale, since one of the widely circulating legends about Menno Simons himself is implicitly erotic, if not also bawdy. The story, which I analyze as a trickster tale in Chapter 4 of the first *MennoFolk* book, says that Menno fell into a barrel of molasses one time when officers of the law interrupted his preaching. He was able to run away and escape only because the quick-witted women who surrounded him proceeded to lick the molasses off his hosen. Even if he sank only up to his thighs—let alone his waist, as some versions claim—the licking of his body parts by female followers is not only bizarre and humorous but also sexually suggestive.

Most of the stories that follow are bawdy, not truly obscene. None of them are profane, meaning that they do not ridicule the Trinity or Godhead. Almost none of them use profane language or blatantly obscene words. Since I did not actively seek out Mennonite stories on taboo subjects, there may be more profane, scatalogically laced stories than I am aware of. But I would guess that the stories printed here embody a certain Mennonite decorum in regard to bawdy tales. That decorum rules out defamation of holy things, using the Name of the Lord in vain, and avoiding the notorious four-letter words.

Once again, Mennonite sensitivities to restrained, careful speech seem to be operative in the content and diction of bawdy story-telling.

Intercourse, Pennsylvania

Mennonites are always amused by the fact that the densely Mennonite and Amish community of Lancaster County, Pennsylvania, harbors a crossroads village named Intercourse. Intercourse is near Blue Ball. And Intercourse and Blue Ball are on the road to Paradise.

A major Mennonite-Amish information center, The People's Place, owned by Mennonites, was formerly located in Intercourse.

No wonder, then, that the most often repeated bawdy story in my collection capitalizes on that in-group knowledge. Here it is, in a form that combines two versions to create a more coherent variant:

> I heard this one a long time ago, and it is an Amish joke. An Amish man was riding through a town with his horse and buggy and he realized he needed to make a pit stop. But he just couldn't get out of the buggy in town. So he saw a bowling alley and he decided, "Well, I'll have to go in there and use their rest room." He went in there and, as he was standing at the urinal, a bowler came in and stood side of him. The bowler didn't know quite what to say, but finally he said: "I'm a little stiff. From bowling." And the Amish man replied: "Glad to meet you. I'm Chris Stoltzfus. From Intercourse." To which the bowler replied: "Oh, I know that. Now where are you from?"

More often, the story is told about a Mennonite man rather than an Amish man, perhaps because Mennonites travel more. The Mennonite is sometimes J. C. Wenger sitting in a restaurant, or an unnamed Mennonite riding in a train or sitting in a bus station beside a stranger. The surprising thing is the number of versions in my collection that mess up the bawdy pun implied by the conjunction of being *stiff* from *Intercourse*. Readers will also notice in this version the assumption that the typical Amishman from Lancaster County is named Stoltzfus, as in the Stoltzfus Factory story. A variant of the story was published by Elmer L. Smith in his *Pennsylvania Dutch Folklore* (20), although using arthritis instead of bowling and New Holland instead of Intercourse, hence lacking the bawdy twist.

Sex and the Amish

Giving the Intercourse story an Amish context is not surprising, considering the number of short Amish stories, told by Mennonites, that reveal a fascination with the sex lives of Amish couples. They probably are related to a certain sexual ambiguity or ambivalence that Amish culture projects to the world in regard to sexuality. On the one hand, the Amish radiate very little sexuality in their public appearances, thanks to their plain, shapeless clothing that is, in part, intended to mute the sexual appeal of their bodies. On the other hand, the Amish have very large families—in northern Indiana, an average of seven children—which indicates that the Amish certainly do not abstain from sexual intercourse.

A host of stories illustrate this outsider's fascination with the possibility of sexual intercourse by Amish people.

> Instead of spending their first wedded night at a friend's house, as is the Amish custom, a newlywed Amish couple decided to stay overnight at a motel. When they arrived there and asked for a room, the desk clerk asked: "Suite?" The man thought that sounded good, so he said, "Yes." Then, "Bridal?" "Oh, no, that's not necessary," the husband said. "I'll just hold her by the ears until she settles down."

The narrator is self-consciously aware that, in putting his Amish couple in a motel, his story does not fit an almost universally practiced custom by Amish newlyweds. The joke may come from elsewhere, but it fits the Amish context because the husband uses images that come from horse-taming culture—like the story told earlier in the book where the new husband threatens with "That's one!"

> An Amish woman was being interviewed by a doctor who asked her if she had ever been bedridden. "Yes," she said, "many times. And even twice in a buggy."

An Amish couple married, but were told to abstain from intercourse for three weeks. Two weeks later the husband confessed to the bishop. They had restrained themselves for two weeks, but then one day his wife bent over to take something off a shelf, and he couldn't stand it, so they went to it right there. "You'll get kicked out of the church for doing that," said the bishop. "Well, I'm not surprised," the Amishman said. "We got kicked out of Krogers."

Amos Herr [fictional name], an Amish farmer in Lancaster County, was busily working around the farmstead when he was visited by a non-Amish person. The visitor noticed a pair of twins with Amos, another pair nearby, and still another pair farther away. Amazed, he asked, "Have you had twins every time?" "Ah-h, no," said Amos. "Tousands and tousands of time we ain't got nothin'."

An Amishman who had already fathered twelve children was asked whether he didn't think that was enough, in light of the population explosion and the problem of feeding the world. "Oh, no," he said. "Sometimes I feel as if I could feed the whole world."

The story is one about the Old Orders [Mennonites]. They have about as many babies as the Amish, you know. So this one morning the mother had had her fifteenth child and had it in the home there. So the neighbor come a-running over and he says, "Abie, I just wanted to see your wife when she wasn't pregnant." And he said, "Aw, you're just fifteen minutes too late!"

In addition to the bridal suite story, others above bear evidence of imperfect adaptation to an Amish context. In the last story, "Abie" suggests a stereotypical Jewish name, rather than Amish (although many Amish men are named Abe). Intercourse in a Kroger aisle would be bizarre for anyone, but even more incredible for Amish people.

And Others

The ancient historical conflict between high church Roman Catholic and low church Mennonite, as seen in the Menno Simons and many other trickster stories, takes on a sexual cast in this story, which also satirizes the Catholic ritual of confession:

> A Catholic priest invited a Mennonite to observe him hear confession and prescribe penance. The first penitent confessed to having had sex with three women since the last confession. The priest prescribed 10 Hail Marys, 10 Our Fathers and 25 cents. Ditto with the second penitent. But then the priest was called away and asked the Mennonite to fill in for him. The third penitent confessed the same sin, except that he had had sex with one woman rather than three. The Mennonite said, "Well, they're three for a quarter this week."

> In my home community in Ontario the Mennonites told this story about an Old Order [Mennonite] farmer. It happened that in a farm accident his horse received a cut of about eight inches long. Not knowing how to handle the wound, he went to the vet for advice. "Put a Kotex as a bandage on it," the vet said. So the Old Order Mennonite went to the store and asked for a box of Kotex. "What size?" asked the salesman. "Well, I don't know," said the Mennonite. "But the cut's this long [demonstrating a twelve-inch length]."

[Mary's] husband, Bill's brother-in-law, was apparently working on the car. He was underneath the car up to his waist. Mary came by and, out of a great sense of humor, she reached down and unzipped his fly and went on into the house. There she found her husband, the pastor, sitting on the table. And she said, "Oh, my God! What have I done?" He said, "I don't know. What have you done?" "I thought that was you out there working on the car." "No," he said, "that's the neighbor I asked to look at…" "Well, I came by and since I thought it was you, I unzipped the trousers." And at that moment the neighbor appeared at the door. And he was bleeding profusely to his forehead. "You'll never believe it, but a moment ago someone unzipped my trousers and," he said, "I tried to sit up under the car." Then he recognized from the shock on her face that it was she! So he solemnly affirmed never to tell anyone. Not to this day!"

This story was told, as a true story, by a very well known Mennonite professional about an equally well known pastoral couple. However, it is definitely a Mennonite variant on a widely distributed American urban legend, named "The Unzipped Plumber or Mechanic" by Jan Brunvand in his book *Encyclopedia of Urban Legends* (ABC CLIO, 2001). The story bears every earmark of urban-legend telling: second-hand reporting, reference to people several steps removed from the narrator, the formulaic "You'll never believe it," and the vow of secrecy. In Chapter 5 of the first *MennoFolk* book I analyze Mennonites' use of the urban legend known as the Elevator Incident, involving three Mennonite women and baseball superstar Reggie Jackson.

A final bawdy story may at first not seem to be Mennonite in any way. However, the punch line will communicate a lot to anyone who recalls the riddle jokes based on the Mennonite family name of *Yoder*:

A man boards an airplane and takes his seat. As he settles in, he glances up and sees the most beautiful woman boarding the plane. He soon realizes she is heading straight towards his seat. A wave of nervous anticipation washes over him. Lo and behold, she takes the seat right beside his. Anxious to strike up a conversation, he blurts out, "So where are you flying to today?"

She turns and smiles and says, "To the annual Nymphomaniac Convention in Chicago."

Whoa! He swallows hard and is instantly crazed with excitement. Here's the most gorgeous woman he has ever seen, sitting right next to him, and she's going to a meeting of nymphomaniacs! Struggling to maintain his outward cool, he calmly asks, "And what's your role at this convention?"

She flips her hair back, turns to him, locks onto his eyes and says, "Well, I try to debunk some of the popular myths about sexuality."

"Really?" he says, swallowing hard. "And what myths are those?"

She explains: "Well, one popular myth is that African-American men are the most well-endowed, when in fact it is the Native American who is most likely to possess this trait. Another popular myth is that Frenchmen are the best lovers, when actually it is Mennonite men who romance women best, on average."

"Very interesting!" the man responds.

Suddenly, the woman becomes very embarrassed and blushes. "I'm sorry," she says. "I feel so awkward discussing this with you. And I don't even know your name."

The man extends his hand and replies, "Tonto. Tonto Yoder."

Gordon Yoder. Yoder Dame. Toyoder. Deyoderized. Kunte Yoder. And now Tonto Yoder.

Yes, The Gordon Principle is at work here, adding a Mennonite label to a joke from mainstream culture. The pairing of key words might just as well be Polish-Kowalski or Irish-O'Reilley or Jewish- Goldberg— all of which any assimilated American would recognize and enjoy. But only a Mennonite would catch on and laugh at the utterance of the final word Yoder, knowing that it referred to a Mennonite.

The story, if told in public, would be offensive to a Mennonite audience because it assumes sex outside of marriage and exploits ethnic and racial stereotypes. But I suspect it represents other such stories told by Mennonites in private, intimate situations.

· EIGHT ·

Personal Legends: Formation

A PERSONAL LEGEND (or "anecdote") is a story attached to an individual and believed to be true. The more prominent the person, the more stories are likely to be told about him or her. For instance, in the United States, more legends are told about Abraham Lincoln than about anyone else.

Because the person named in the legend is historical, the hearer initially is disposed to believe in the historical truth of the story. But the relationship of personal legend to personal history is a complex, and often dubious one, thanks to the tendencies in oral storytelling by which personal legends are passed on and sustained over time. This chapter will examine the relationship between the legend transmission process and history, in order to prepare the reader to be a better audience for the Mennonite personal legends that will appear in the final two chapters.

Variant Forms

Even if the origin of a story can be traced to a historical time and place, the oral transmission of a story over time will have created narrative versions that vary in small or large details. Even when people who "were there and saw it" tell the same story, it will vary in details from teller to teller.

Two personal legends about Mennonite relief efforts in Europe following World War 2 will illustrate this tendency. Although they are very modest stories, their variants arouse heated discussions about historicity among people who worked in Europe and knew the people involved. The legends may be of marginal interest to other people, but they illustrate the key folklore principle of "multiple and variant forms" and reveal some interesting things about the obsessions of the very human relief workers who nurtured the legends.

One of the stories concerns Harold S. Bender (1897-1962), a sometimes intimidating mover and shaker in Mennonite domestic and foreign circles following the war. Atlee (1915-2001) and Winifred Nelson (1915-2001) Beechy were life-long peace activists in the Mennonite Church, beginning with their service in Basel, Switzerland, following the end of World War 2.

> After World War 2, Atlee Beechys were at the [Mennonite Central Committee] unit house and the evening meal was always very formal. Napkins and all. And H. S. Bender came through one time and ate with us that evening—eating and talking. And as soon as he finished the plate, he just reached over and got a piece of pie and put it on his plate and started eating. Karen, the oldest daughter, was sitting there, and she looked over at him and she said, "Here we wait until we are all finished."

But another person who was also there says,

> "We were there! And it wasn't pie! The punch line that Karen said, because her mother was out in the kitchen doing a few things yet, was, "We always wait till Winnie comes back."

In his journal entry that describes the event, Atlee Beechy—feeling no obligation to tell a good story—vindicates the former version and adds elements of his own:

> April 8, 1948. Karen seems to have special respect for two MCC workers, H. S. Bender and C. F. Klassen [1894-1954]. She always uses Brother Bender or Brother Klassen when addressing them. The rest of the large MCC family are called by their first names. Karen's special respect was tested this evening when she noticed that Bender started eating his dessert as soon as it was served to him. Karen, uninhibited and unafraid as three and a half-year olds are, called down the long table, "Brother Bender, we wait until everyone is served before eating our dessert." Winifred's face reflected a mixture of surprise and shock as probably mine did too. Before we could say anything Brother Bender replied, "You are so right, Karen. I'm sorry, and I thank you for reminding me." It was good to see this human side of Harold. I wish more people could see this side of him. *Seeking Peace: My Journey* [2001], p. 33.

The first two tellings of this event, by relief workers, stop short with Karen's blunt admonition to the revered Brother Bender, creating a punch-line that is a kind of proverbial reprimand for him. Atlee's version goes one step farther by quoting Bender's response and illustrating his graciousness. Atlee sees the "human side" of Bender; the relief workers emphasize his more commonly perceived colder side and satirize it. The retelling of the story has shaped it into a narrative with a punchline climax, as opposed to Atlee's more diffused version.

The Bender story bears an uncanny resemblance to a similar one told about Orie O. Miller (1892-1977), another prominent leader in

Mennonite relief circles in Europe immediately following World War 2. The story also concerns his table manners at dessert time.

> Orie Miller was visiting somewhere among the Dutch Mennonites in the early days of MCC in Europe. It was in the time immediately after the war—reconstruction—and so sugar was in short supply—desserts were in short supply and sweets were in short supply. Orie and some MCC people were being entertained, and the Dutch hostess had very carefully counted out the exact number of cookies, so that there would be one cookie for everyone who was there. And then when it came around to Orie, Orie said, "I'll take two now, so it doesn't have to be passed a second time." And then the story that circulated among some of the PAX men after that was: "Take two. Orie does."

The punch line, "Take two. Orie does," became a proverb that Mennonite relief workers in Europe loved to use: "Our unit picked this up, and used it as a general saying at any or all occasions when something relatively scarce was being passed around."

However, another version of the story says that it happened not in Holland but in Basel, Switzerland—around the dinner table of Atlee and Winifred Beechy. In that variant, the first person to utter "Take two. Orie does" was their oldest daughter Karen. The Beechy family has no recollection of O. O. Miller taking two cookies. The cookie story must have happened elsewhere—*perhaps* in Holland—but the dominant position of the Beechy family in Basel and the familiarity of the pie (was it?) story has apparently attracted the Miller story to the Bender story's milieu.

Why did such little, homey stories became so compelling for Mennonite relief workers engaged in heroic efforts in difficult situations? Both stories bring down to a more human level O. O. Miller and H. S.

Bender, who were revered, towering presences and the relief workers' superiors. Both stories also reveal the relief workers' reverent—even obsessive—attitudes toward food (in scarce postwar supply), and especially toward desserts, which were luxuries because they required sugar. Both also show an understandable human anxiety about maintaining ordinary social decorum in the midst of the chaos of postwar reconstruction.

The *facts* of these personal legends may be in dispute, but the *truth* that radiates from the narratives makes them socially valuable—and therefore believable.

Migratory Legends

In the cookies legend, the subject moves from someone in Holland to Atlee and Winifred Beechy in Switzerland. Such movement of a story from one person to another illustrates the *migratory* nature of many legends. They can be attached to different people or places depending on the narrator's memory—or purpose. Thus do legends become fictionalized versions of presumed history.

Legends of the underground railroad or of haunted houses, for instance, tend to cluster around the most imposing old houses in a community. And stories about people tend to migrate to the most prominent people on the historical or current social horizon. As mentioned earlier, in mainstream American culture, the best example in personal legends is Abraham Lincoln, who is probably the best-known historical figure for Americans. Although Lincoln led a rich life, it could not possibly embrace all of the varied incidents and statements attributed to him in the folk tradition.

This principle of prominence is illustrated in the cookie legend, where the subject migrates to a family that was very prominent in the lives of Mennonite relief workers in Europe. In American Mennonite culture at large, the most personal legends are told about prominent leaders like J. C. Wenger, John Howard Yoder (1928-1998), H. S.

Bender and Orie O. Miller, although many obviously come from other sources and have merely become attached—that is, have *migrated*—to these Mennonites.

A good illustration of this folklore principle is a story told about C. F. Derstine (1891-1967) of Kitchener, Ontario, who was a popular evangelist and preached in many Mennonite communities in the U.S. and Canada.

> C. F. Derstine always would tell the story about when he held meetings down in the hillbilly country of Kentucky. And he looked out in the kitchen and he saw the woman of the house getting the dinner and she was lifting the stove lid and spitting in this fire, and she picked up a piece of wood out of the woodbox and was mashing the potatoes. He saw all this going on and by that time his stomach was getting sort of queasy. And so when it came time to go to the table, he asked the lady of the house whether she'd make him a soft-boiled egg. (variant in Barrick 32-33)

Because the narrator had heard Derstine tell this story about himself "for gospel truth," she was surprised and disappointed when she read a similar anecdote in *Reader's Digest* and realized that the evangelist was using a traditional story and applying it to himself. Other versions circulating in the U.S. might have the cook spitting into the soup instead of the fire, as well as include a third disgusting culinary offense to add to the other two.

Mennonites, who treasure truth-telling as implied by Matthew 5:37, might indeed be shocked by such casual disregard for truth. But another anecdote shows another Mennonite leader giving himself aesthetic and moral leeway in fictionalizing his own experience.

John C. Wenger (1910-1995), as mentioned before, was a conservative historian, theologian and preacher who always wore the plain coat, long after it was no longer required for ordained men. In a series of special meetings that he conducted at the New Paris, Indiana, Church of the Brethren, he told a story of how he was stopped for speeding on the turnpike and mistaken for a Catholic priest by the patrolman, who forgave him and waved him on. (See Chapter 3, "More Trickster Tales.") Although he must have given some hedged comments regarding the truth of the story, he was asked following the meeting whether it really happened. J. C. replied, "I'll never tell you."

The shifty nature of legends, as illustrated by variants and migration, undermines their authority only insofar as actual history is concerned. If an audience can tolerate ambiguity in the amount of belief to give a legend, they will find other values that are just as important. All personal legends are "true" insofar as they communicate ideas about their subjects that ring "true" to their character or mission, or that reflect what their audience perceived to be "true" about them.

Legend Formation

The way that historical experience becomes transformed and fictionalized into legend in the Mennonite community can be illustrated by a story that I was able to trace from its beginning through a number of levels of transmission, including the original narrator. We might regard these as "degrees of separation" in the grapevine. Folklorists call it the *folklore conduit*.

Although, for a time, this personal legend was a compelling narrative in oral circulation, it has not remained in the repertoire of Mennonite storytellers through the years. That is a bit surprising since the hero of the story remains prominent in Mennonite circles and the story itself embodies the glamorous allure of a Mennonite coming into contact with a "star" from mainstream culture—a motif that frequently captivates Mennonite narrators and audiences.

The story unfolding below is about an actual experience by June Alliman Yoder of Goshen, Indiana, and her friends in 1987. I will give her version of it—presumably the authoritative one—in full, but then only parts of re-tellings of the event by (1) another person who was there and saw and heard it, (2) two persons who heard the story from someone who was there, (3) someone who heard the story third-hand and (4) a narrator yet farther removed from the original telling. June Yoder is a colorful, well-known Mennonite preacher and public speaker, now retired from teaching homiletics at Anabaptist Mennonite Biblical Seminary in Elkhart, Indiana.

First step in conduit: June Yoder's Version

There were eight of us (four couples) traveling to Chicago from Goshen in a van. We were on our way for an evening out—dinner and the theater. On the [Indiana] toll road we stopped at the last rest plaza before you leave Indiana and go into Illinois. The men went to their restroom and we four women went to ours.

When we got inside the restroom, it appeared we were the only ones there, so we continued our lighthearted, jovial banter while each one found a stall. As I went into my stall I noticed that in the stall next to mine there was a large black woman. The stall door was open and she was standing there, facing the toilet. I saw only her back, but noticed that she had on blue jeans, a sweatshirt and a baseball cap. The door open, facing the toilet, dressed like that—I assumed she must be cleaning or working in there.

As I sat down, my ear noticed that the woman was humming. Still feeling playful, I decided, "Heck, if she can hum, I can sing!" So I broke out in a loud, robust "Somewhere Over the Rainbow . . .." The hard tile walls of the restroom gave it the full vibration of a shower stall virtuoso.

Soon one of my friends finished and left her stall. She was immediately encountered by the woman asking, "Are

Personal Legends: Formation

you the person with the full, rich, soprano voice?"

"No," she said, and went to wash her hands.

A second friend came out and again she was approached: "Was that you with the beautiful, rich, soprano voice?"

"No, it wasn't me," she also replied.

As I sat in my seclusion I thought to myself, "What kind of kook do we have on our hands?" But I decided to go out and "face the music"! So I emerged from my stall to be met with the same energized "Was that you with the beautiful, rich, soprano voice?"

Being scared and embarrassed and proud all at the same time, I mumbled, "Yes, that was me doing the singing, but I didn't mean to disturb anyone. Please excuse me. My friends and I are on our way to a show in Chicago and I was just feeling light and happy."

"Oh, so you are with a choir," she replied.

"No, we're just friends going to Chicago to see a show."

"Oh, but you must be singers. I know good voices when I hear them. My friend Leontyne Price and I know good soprano voices."

While this conversation was happening, we were all washing and drying our hands—no one knowing what to do or who was in charge. But at that moment one person's eyes lit up. She had been watching [The Phil] Donahue [Show] that week and Leontyne Price was the guest. She spoke of things she liked to do with her friend Pearl Bailey.

So my friend says cautiously, "Are you Pearl Bailey?"

"Yes, I am."

She was on her way to Chicago for preparation work for a performance she had scheduled there. We visited briefly. She gave us all signed pictures of herself and we left the rest room together. As we left the rest room, our husbands were waiting for us. Seeing the men, she said, "You are with a choir?" (It's a shame we didn't try to sing "606" for her!)

We introduced her to our husbands and she introduced us to her chauffeur.

June Alliman Yoder is a fine story-teller, so her account is detailed and coherent. One might suspect some doctoring of the event, already, since the sequence of women being interrogated by Pearl Bailey is three-fold, which is a classic convention in folk narrative performance.

First step in conduit

The account by a second woman in the rest room confirms everything in June Yoder's account. It omits some of the details, but remembers a number of other striking elements that June omitted:

> ...On our way to Chicago to see a play or the Bolshoi Ballet... We three women (Was there a fourth? I can't recall.) ...a black woman wearing a baseball hat—Georgetown U. Hoyas... Maybe we started singing along [with June]... The woman added, "Leontyne Price is my friend."... as we were about to leave the bathroom, Libby blurted out: "Are you Pearl Bailey?"... There ensued a 5-10 minute conversation, including the men.... She said she hates to fly. ...when we were in line to buy tickets at the theater I saw a poster announcing her show. We passed her Cadillac and tooted once or twice. They waved back. We laughed all the way to Chicago and back.

Second step in conduit

One narrator tells a version based on what she heard from June Yoder herself:

Personal Legends: Formation

> ...June assumed she was the cleaning lady....At this point in the story, June says, she realizes it is Pearl Bailey. She had a hat on like P. B. wears....the women introduced Pearl Bailey to their husbands. There may have been others there with them, too. I don't remember that part. After Pearl Bailey saw the group she said, "See, you are with a choir!"... Together they all waited. I don't remember what for.

This is a very condensed and hesitant re-telling of the story. It makes only a few changes—June, not Libby, first recognizes Pearl Bailey—and adds no truly new details.

Third step in conduit: Variant A

A retelling of the event in a third step of the conduit—heard from the second-step narrator cited above—is interesting enough to be quoted in full, since it shows many variances from the original narrated version. Some additions and changes are underlined in order to highlight variant elements.

> Oh, did you hear the experience June Yoder had? She and Shirley Showalter and Judith Davis were attending a meeting in Washington, D. C. and after lunch they went to use the rest room. Judith went into the first empty stall and Shirley went into the next one she found empty and June walked on down toward the end and went into the next to last one.
>
> In the very last one (the stall for the handicapped) the door was open and a rather large lady was moving around in there, humming and sort of clanging—possibly changing clothes, June wasn't sure—but just humming all the while.
>
> Well, June recognized the hymn she was humming and, in typical June fashion, began singing right along, singing quite heartily as she took care of her business.

> While the women were washing their hands, the large lady finally finished whatever she was doing and came on out of her stall. She asked Shirley if she had been singing, then asked Judith if she was the one with the good voice.
>
> When she found out it was June, she asked her if she had ever auditioned. June laughingly thanked her but indicated modestly that she'd grown up in a tradition of singing and just loved to sing.
>
> Well, the lady insisted her voice had potential and that she wanted her good friend Leontyne Price—who was waiting outside the door—to hear her sing.
>
> The large lady was Pearl Bailey.

Although most of the additions and changes in this version do not affect the story, three of them do. One interesting change in content is that Leontyne Price is present and not merely referred to by Pearl Bailey. Also June's "Somewhere Over the Rainbow" is replaced with a hymn tune, which the Mennonite context—especially the many references to "singing in a choir"—would naturally lead to. The major change in form is that the story ends with a punch line—"The large lady was Pearl Bailey."—for a dramatic climax, as one would expect from a fictional as opposed to a historical account.

Third step in conduit: Variant B

Another person in the third step of the conduit heard his version from the same source as the second-step narrator. Only the significant phrases are retained.

> ... (The third [woman] might have been Judith Davis instead) were at some unidentified conference ... So when June comes out, she is vigorously accosted and praised for her wonderful voice. Woman identifies herself as either

Personal Legends: Formation

Pearl Bailey or Leontyne Price and invites her to go out and see the other one of the two named, and their husbands. They do, have an exchange of addresses, etc.

This extremely condensed version is interesting mainly because of what it does with Leontyne Price, who was mentioned in the original encounter and then became present in the third-step version cited above. Here the narrator's uncertainty over which of the two was in the restroom considerably weakens the impact and meaning of the story. But it shows the legend beginning to *migrate* in the direction of making Leontyne Price the main character, rather than Pearl Bailey.

Fourth (or more) step in conduit

One more conduit step and several years removed from the event, a third very young narrator learned her version from a different, also very young, second-step source.

> I heard that maybe four or five years ago. June Yoder was traveling with her family to Chicago. ... June was in one of the stalls, humming. She then started singing "606." A voice from the woman in the stall next to her called, "Who is that singing?"
>
> June stopped singing and didn't respond, as she was embarrassed—or so I am told. June is actually not one to get embarrassed easily. Anyway, June waited a little longer in the stall until she thought the woman might be gone. She was washing her hands when the black woman next to her at the sink asked ... The other women complimented her, saying she had a lovely voice. They chatted a little bit and June introduced herself.
>
> As it turned out, the other woman was Pearl Bailey! Pearl went with June to meet June's family. Then Pearl got back

into her limousine...and June got back into their small car
...Pearl had given them some autographed pictures before
parting. On the highway they passed each other a couple of
times and waved back and forth each time.

June is much more passive in this account, and, for the first time, we learn that Pearl Bailey traveled in a limousine and June (with family, not friends) drove a "small car." Most surprising, is what has happened to June's "Somewhere Over the Rainbow." It not only becomes a hymn here, as it did in the 3.A variant, but it becomes "606"—which June referred to in passing in her first-hand account. "606" is playfully known by Mennonites as "the Mennonite national anthem." Published in 1830 by the Boston Handel and Haydn Society, it is an anthemic version of the doxology, "Praise God from Whom All Blessings Flow." It first appeared in Mennonite circles as hymn number 606 in *The Mennonite Hymnal* (1969). It is very difficult to sing, but many Mennonite congregations sing it in unaccompanied four-part harmony from memory. It is the hymn that Mennonites will most likely sing during a large assembly, or as a communal greeting or farewell for a special guest (e.g., Garrison Keillor at Goshen College in 2015)—as June herself alludes to in her first-hand account. In *Hymnal: A Worship Book* (1992), which succeeded *The Mennonite Hymnal,* the hymn has become number 118. But it is still referred to more often as "606" than by either its title or its new number—which shows its full integration into Mennonite folk culture.

If a Mennonite did not know the people involved, the "Mennonite" content of the legend would be clear from June's family name, *Yoder.* But the even more esoteric knowledge is of "606," which only Mennonites would recognize. So this last variant becomes the first version of the legend to carry an unambiguously "Mennonite" tribal meaning.

· NINE ·

Personal Legends: George Brunk, Sr.

GEORGE R. BRUNK, SR. (1871-1938) was a charismatic leader of a segment of the Mennonite Church that objected to the corroding influence of "modernism" and rival liberal theologies on traditional Mennonite beliefs and practices. Coming mainly from the conservative Virginia Conference, centered on Eastern Mennonite College (now University) in Harrisonburg, Virginia, they waged a vigorous campaign to restore the church, by presenting public programs throughout American Mennonite communities and by sponsoring the periodical *Sword and Trumpet* (1927-1938),which was overtly controversialist.

When George R. Brunk, Sr., died in 1938, Ernest G. Gehman (1901-1988) assembled an issue devoted to the memory of Brunk. Gehman, who taught German at Eastern Mennonite College, was Brunk's closest associate and Office Editor of *Sword and Trumpet*. He also contributed over thirty editorial cartoons to *Sword and Trumpet*.

The July 1938 memorial issue included the sermon preached at Brunk's funeral by J. J. Stauffer, Associate Editor; an essay on "Balanced Truth Bridling the Tongue" by R. J. Shank; and articles by Brunk, the most interesting being "Supernatural Guidance," which recounts a series of supernatural experiences from throughout his life. The concluding memorial section of the issue is entitled, "George R. Brunk as I Knew Him," and contains personal appreciations and remembrances of him by twenty-seven of his followers from throughout the United States.

The issue concludes with "Revealing Incidents from the Life of Geo. R. Brunk," written by Ernest G. Gehman and consisting of seventeen pithy, unlinked anecdotes with Brunk as the central figure. They, along with scattered anecdotes in the appreciations by other followers, constitute a very revealing series—the folkloristic term is *cycle*—of personal legends about this charismatic leader. All of the anecdotes quoted in this essay illustrate the importance that the well chosen word or phrase—the *bon mot*—played in his ministry and in inspiring his followers. The anecdotes are published here with the permission of Gehman's descendants.

Traditional African-American culture gives an honored place to the "man of words," whether as preacher or rap artist. Traditional American Mennonite culture has honored the "man of words" in the social roles as preacher, song-leader or auctioneer. George R. Brunk was a special kind of Mennonite man of words as he carried out his calling as an evangelist, Bible teacher and controversialist. His forceful use of words fulfills the controversialist mission of *Sword of Trumpet*, but it departs dramatically from traditional Mennonite norms for the spoken word.

Man of Words

In his biography of Brunk, *Faithfully, Geo. R.* (Harrisonburg, VA 1978), J. C. Wenger points out that he was "hated by liberals, loved by conservatives, feared by those who differed with him, and respected by those who had the insight to grasp the convictions by which he lived" (99). Brunk would have regarded that description as a compliment.

Two of his followers, writing in *Sword and Trumpet,* suggested how that reputation was created and supported by his forceful use of words. As R. J. Shenk put it, "Bro. Brunk was a man who did not care for a lot of 'small talk,' and was therefore not known to use many unnecessary words, did not believe in flattering . . . He said what he meant and meant what he said, for he was a man of strong and settled convictions" (67). J. B. Smith said it more forcefully: ". . . in the field of controversy and in combating error Bro. Brunk was bold as a lion . . . His logic was inexorable and irresistible. If one admitted the correctness of his major premises he might just as well admit his conclusions . . . for Geo. R. would be likely to apply the force of his keen wit and thus laugh him out of court" (*S&T* 71). A good example of Brunk's witty invective is his evaluation of the heresies of Modernism and Darwinism: "Such doctrines are no more Christian than a stinking carcass-eating buzzard is a dove" (*Faithfully* 153).

Brunk was aware of the aggressive nature of his language. He relished it, and gave a biblical and theological rationale for it:

> Bro. Brunk's presence at meetings and conferences where liberals were in the ascendancy was often embarrassing to them. On one occasion they sought to dispose of the problem by giving him the subject of "Love" to speak on. When his subject was announced he arose and spoke somewhat as follows: "The brethren have asked me to speak on love. It is needless for me to tell you the many nice things that you all know about love. But I want to call your attention to a phase of love that is not often emphasized. My text is the words of Jesus, 'As many as I love I rebuke and chasten' and my theme is the fact that love carries a stick!" (78)

Most of the anecdotes in Gehman's list follow the pattern of the one just cited: they present a context, a challenger, a challenge, and a retort by Brunk that sounds like the last word on the subject. They illustrate Brunk's motto: "Love carries a stick." And they tend to laugh the challenger "out of court," as J. B. Smith said above.

To Brunk's credit, one anecdote that concludes with "a word fitly spoken" but is not a putdown concerns his attitude as a southerner to African-Americans:

> Once he was asked to address a multitude of Negroes in a large auditorium. He began by saying, "Sometimes people ask, 'Who is the better man—the white man or the colored man?' I'll tell you the answer to that: the colored man is the better man—if he is a better man; and the white man is the better man if he is a better man." It was sometime before he could continue speaking because of the prolonged applause that followed this statement which rightly divided men—on the basis of inner rather than outer conditions. (S&P 77-78)

Two other stories about Brunk's early life conclude with witty statements lacking moral or theological points. They survive in a typescript in the Goshen Archives of Mennonite Church USA, apparently written by Gehman. Perhaps he left them out of the memorial issue because they are merely funny, not edifying:

> When Mennonite settlement was being considered at Protection, Kansas, early in this century, George, R. J. Heatwole, and Henry E. Hostetler went to Wichita, and contacted a real estate firm. Accompanied by a land agent they boarded a train for Protection. Upon arriving at Protection they secured a livery rig and toured Comanche County. On one occasion after the agent had given a high powered sales talk, George remarked, "Heatwole believes everything you say, I believe half of it, and Hostetler doesn't believe any of it." [ms 1]

In spite of George R. Brunk's remark to the land agent, he and Henry E. Hostetler purchased farms, and moved to Protection in 1907. However, crops were uncertain, and they both became fearful of the future in Western Kansas, which is about one-hundred miles east of Protection, in 1909. After this George frequently remarked to his friend Henry Hostetler, "The difference between Protection and Harper is that at Harper it rains fifteen minutes before it is too late, and at Protection it rains fifteen minutes after it is too late." [ms 1-2]

Brunk Vs. Opponents

However, most of the stories consisting of context, challenger, challenge and retort conclude with sharp, pithy moral judgments. The anecdotes become joke-like because they end with punchlines that are sardonic and darkly humorous.

The first issue of *Sword and Trumpet* announced that its targets would be "liberalism and Calvinism" and people of "old Goshen" (151). By *liberalism* Brunk meant the modernist questioning of the life of Christ and the authority of scripture. By *Calvinism* he meant any version of Christianity that limited the free will of humans, Brunk being an Arminian. By *old Goshen* Brunk meant modernist Mennonite tendencies as found at Goshen College before it was closed by conservatives in 1923 (then reorganized and reopened in 1924). The anecdotes quoted below—all except one are taken from the memorial issue—condemn liberalism and Calvinism, although not old Goshen. His holy scorn ranges widely and often strikes hapless individuals, not only groups or doctrines.

Against indecorous conduct
A medical-college student was carrying the dismembered finger of a dead woman around in his pocket and hav-

ing some "fun," as he called it, with the younger people. Bro. Brunk remonstrated with him. The student said: "It's nothing; the finger of a dead woman isn't anything." Bro. Brunk then asked, "Wouldn't it be anything either if your mother were dead and someone were carrying one of her fingers around?" The student saw the point and the ill-chosen jesting ceased. (78)

Against superstition

He was always impatient with superstitions and in the days before hotels discontinued placing the number 13 on any of their rooms, he would ask to be given room number 13. Once also when he had said to someone that he was thinking of beginning to build a house on a certain day, the man was startled and said, "Why, that's on a Friday! It's always bad luck to start anything on Friday."

"Well," replied Bro. Brunk, "just to prove to you that such superstitions are foolish I'm going to be sure to start on that very day." And he did! (77)

In a certain congregation the men's Bible class frequently had to suffer the lengthy recital of dreams by one of the members who attached a religious importance to all his dreams. One day Bro. Brunk was present and the man took special time and pain to impress the distinguished visitor. Bro. Brunk sized up the situation at once and at the end of the boresome rehearsal he merely commented, "Some people wouldn't dream so much if they wouldn't eat mince-pie for supper." It is reported that thereafter the Sunday-school class had relief from dream-telling. (78-89)

Against Calvinists

Once when Bro. Brunk had been speaking words of comfort to a brother ill in an open ward in a hospital, he turned to another man on a bed nearby and asked of the state of his soul. The man, reflecting his Calvinistic teaching, gruffly replied, "If God wants me let Him come and get me!"

"Listen," said Brother Brunk, "if you don't concern yourself about your soul's salvation and do something about it, somebody will come and get you, and it won't be God, either!" (77)

Once a Baptist friend visiting in the Mennonite colony commented on the fine-looking and bountiful farms and orchards there and said, "It seems as if the Lord shows special favors to the Mennonites."

"Not so," said Bro. Brunk, "but you Calvinists are trying to raise crops by faith only, while we believe and practice a proper combination of faith and works." (77)

Against Catholics

A Catholic woman in the market one day told Bro. Brunk how she fasts before the eucharist (communion)—"so that I can keep Christ in my body as long as possible."

"That's where the Catholics differ from the Mennonites," said Bro. Brunk; "we take Christ into our hearts, not into our stomachs!" (77)

To another Catholic who was justifying their praying to Jesus' mother, he said, "Why don't you pray to Jesus' grandmother, too?" (77)

Against Atheists
Robert G. Ingersoll (1833-1899) was a famous lawyer, orator and avowed atheist.

> Once after a sermon in which Bro. Brunk denounced the infidelity of men like Robert G. Ingersoll, a brother came to him and wondered whether it was all right to buy Ingersoll watches. Bro. Brunk smiled and said, "Certainly; Ingersoll will do for time but not for eternity" (78).

Likely, this clever play on words was a widespread proverb among fundamentalists of Brunk's day, attributed to him here but not actually coined by him.

Against Modernizing Mennonites
On the occasion of a conference in Canada, Bro. Brunk and a Mennonite College president were traveling thither in the same railway coach. It was not a great while before this man's final defection from the faith and he bitterly denounced regulation religious garb, among other things, and declared it a meaningless and useless form. Bro. Brunk spoke equally strongly in defence of it. As the train stopped at the Canadian border the order went through the coaches that everyone should lay his baggage open for the customary inspection . . . When the officer came down the aisle he looked at Bro. Brunk and pushed his suitcase shut without a second glance at it, but he pawed completely through the contents of the college president's luggage, much to the mortification of the latter. Bro. Brunk looked at the man meaningfully and said, "Did you say there was nothing in plain clothes?" (78)

Notice here another variant on the plain-coat preacher-trickster story.

> During the earlier days of his ministry Brother Brunk wore a long dress coat. On one occasion he visited a section of the church where neck ties were being worn. While in the community he preached against ties. Later some of the brethren took him to task for wearing a long coat. To this he replied, "I guess I ought to cut the tail off and make some more neckties for you fellows." [ms 2]

The Power of the Word

The efficacy of Brunk's spoken word is demonstrated by the positive moral and spiritual effects that his retorts bring about. But Brunk's verbal success is explained, appreciated and magnified by what is implied by his son's recollection of the power of Brunk's words in prayer to God:

> Different people have remarked that when Bro. Brunk prayed he seemed to be talking right to God. But it would be better to eliminate the word "seemed" and say that he talked right to God. When he prayed he did not attempt to impress his human hearers but he spoke to God in terms and tones of humble and respectful intimacy used by a child when addressing its earthly father in grateful or pleading tones. And the Lord answered his prayers.
>
> When physicians and friends despaired of his life twenty years ago he felt that his work was so incomplete and that his wife and little children needed him so much that he prayed definitely for his restoration to health. Then two years ago when he was equally ill things seemed different (as the last letter quoted by Bro. Maynard Hoover makes

clear) and he told Sister Brunk that he did not feel impelled to pray for his return to health this time—that he would let the Lord's will be made plain in the matter. But his companion earnestly and tearfully pleaded with him that for her sake and for the children's sake he should again pray for recovery. This he finally did and was restored to health.

Now one of the sons, in relating these facts, said that he believes that this time the Lord took him to Himself suddenly and unexpectedly [by heart attack] so that there was no opportunity for him to pray otherwise. "For," said he, "I know that when my father prayed, the Lord heard him. And it seems as if this time He really wanted him to go." (79)

Of structural interest here is that the narrative is shaped with three different occasions of prayer in Brunk's life. In the first two, he prayed and God answered his prayers. In the third, God took him before he could pray. The three-fold sequence illustrates again typical folklore formation. Of thematic interest here is that Brunk's way with words is so spiritually powerful that God cannot help but listen and answer the prayers. In fact, God's only means of getting his way with George Brunk is to give him a heart attack or stroke with so immediate an effect that Brunk had not even a moment to pray and charm God into saving his life. Such presumed control of God by a man represents the ultimate in Arminianism. This darkly humorous story makes of Brunk an even greater spiritual warrior, or man of words, than the earlier stories do. Appropriately, Gehman prints it last in his series of anecdotes.

The Word as Sword

Of course, one problem with this use of stories about George Brunk, Sr., is that all of them come from a compilation that appeared in print, not from tape-recorded oral performances of them, which folklorists prefer. Although I am convinced that the stories must have, at minimum, constituted Ernest G. Gehman's personal repertoire of oral narratives about Brunk, I can only assume and assert without other evidence that they circulated widely among the disciples in his community of dissent. Perhaps their structural similarity, and their obsession with forceful words, reveals more about Gehman himself than about Brunk and his followers. For instance, other contributors to the memorial issue recount stories that reveal a more sympathetic, tender spirit in Brunk.

However, one important consideration that connects their structure and content to the historical George Brunk, Sr. comes from the title and meaning of his publication *Sword and Trumpet*. The masthead of the periodical indicates that the "Sword" of the title comes from the Bible verse, "Take the Sword of the Spirit which is the Word of God" (Eph. 6:17). Both Brunk and Gehman used the word as a sword—even a two-edged sword—in doctrinal battle. The "Trumpet" of the title comes from the Bible verse, "Blow ye the Trumpet and warn the people" (Eze. 33:3). Like a trumpet, Gehman's stories about Brunk are loud, aggressive and confident in their moral clarity. The visual logo of the magazine—no doubt drawn by Gehman, whose elaborate moral allegorical cartoons adorn the publication—is an ominous arrangement of a Bible lying atop a crossed sword and trumpet, yielding this motto: "The weapons of our warfare are not carnal but mighty through God to the pulling down of strongholds" (2 Cor. 10:4). And the overall mission statement says that *Sword and Trumpet* is "Devoted to the defense of a Full Gospel, with Especial Emphasis upon Neglected Truths and to an Active Opposition to the Various Forms of Error that Contribute to the Religious Drift of the Times." Gehman's stories about Brunk are definitely of a piece with such aggressive notions of the role of the minister in controversial times.

George R. Brunk, Sr., claimed that he was merely calling Mennonites back to their true, traditional ways. What he didn't notice is that he was doing so in a strident voice that he probably borrowed from his controversialist, fundamentalist models in mainstream American Christianity but that was foreign to the quiet, careful, respectful speech that characterized his ancestors and that was restated in the essay "Bridling the Tongue" in the memorial issue.

Like Flannery O'Connor, the American Catholic fiction-writer, George R. Brunk, Sr. apparently thought that, in a spiritually deaf culture, you have to shout loud.

Or blow the trumpet.

· TEN ·

More Personal Legends

ANABAPTIST GROUPS, at their best, hold to the equality of all human beings. Like the Quakers, they tip their hats to no one—or to everyone. They are anti-hierarchical, suspicious of those who would lord it over others. In their fellowships of believers, they cultivate congregationalism and honor the voice of all.

In Amish communities, that ideal is expressed through uniform costume, as well as in cemeteries, where the small gravestones are of equal size, with barely enough room for the deceased's name and life dates. In Mennonite churches, the ideal is expressed by decisions arrived at by consensus, by studies carried out by lay committees, by an increasingly congregational polity, and by a suspicion of charismatic leadership.

But failures to attain the Anabaptist ideal of equality abound. Although the Amish *ordnung* is unique to every local district, not beholden to a national organization, the Amish nevertheless honor—and obey—their bishops and other ordained leaders. In the early twentieth century, Mennonites, too, yielded congregational authority to ordained men and conference regulations, although in recent years church polity has returned to a more democratic governance, albeit one that borrows from American corporate practices.

Especially in the revivalist movement of the late nineteenth and early twentieth centuries, as well as in their increasing activisim during World War 2 and following, Mennonites learned to know and revere certain leaders—usually male—either because of their charismatic spirit (as with evangelist George R. Brunk, Jr.) or because of their amazing accomplishments (as with relief worker Peter Dyck).

However, the stories Mennonites tell about such leaders are almost always humorous and satirical, as if ordinary members feel a need to bring them back down to the level of a common humanity. These *personal legends* are usually told as true by their narrators, and believed to be true by their audience. If readers recall the principles of *multiple and variant forms* in folklore in general and the *migratory* nature of folk tales, they will greet some of these with healthy skepticism as to their historicity.

Preachers and Discipline

Mennonites today tend to ridicule the clothing restrictions that prevailed among them in the U.S. from about 1910 to 1950. The first such legend, about Iowa Amish bishop Christian E. (Chris) Hershberger (1872-1966) highlights the ironies inherent in early attitudes toward dress and tobacco use:

> Back at the turn of the century, five of the Amish-Mennonite bishops [in eastern Iowa] gathered to determine by the discernment process whether they had now reached the point where they would allow pockets to be sewn into the pants. And they spent the morning debating and discussing this. And by the end of the morning they finally turned to one bishop and said, "Brother Chris, what do you think?" And he said, "Well, whether it be right to have pockets in your pants, I cannot say. But I do know this: It sure would be nice to have some place to keep my tobacco!"

Another story about preachers' costumes comes from the Lancaster Mennonite Conference and concerns Lewis C. Good (1899-1978), pastor of the Cottage City, Maryland, congregation. It questions the biblical basis for the Lancaster Conference rule that ministers, unlike laity, had to wear the frock-tail coat, an old-fashioned men's dress style from the nineteenth century:

> [Lewis Good] was wearing a lay-down [lapel] suit. But he was never used in the church where he lived because he was wearing the wrong clothes. He had a straight-cut coat hanging in the closet and couldn't bring himself to wear it. Then one day he decided he was just losing too much time, so he went and he wore it. And then immediately he was made Sunday School superintendent, teacher, and a number of other things. And after a while he was put in the lot twice—once for deacon and once for minister of the church. Every time he was in the lot, the bishops all gathered around and they quizzed him to see whether he was really suitable for the job. He asked one day, "Well, why should I wear a frock-tail coat?" Solemn for a while. Then one of the men spoke up and said, "Well, that's one of the mysteries of the Gospel."

Daniel Brenneman (1834-1919) of near Wakarusa, Indiana, left the Mennonite Church and formed the Mennonite Brethren in Christ Church, later known as the United Missionary Church, now the Missionary Church. Two innovations that Brenneman advocated, in opposition to his home church, were four-part singing and preaching in English rather than German:

> One day Brenneman was walking along the road and a stranger picked him up and they didn't know each other.

And the fellow in the buggy was a Mennonite. So after a bit the Mennonite said to Brenneman, "What do you think of Daniel Brenneman?" And Brenneman sort of excused himself. He said, "Oh, I don't know. What do you?" He said, "Not much! He sings bass and preaches English." That was enough to condemn him. —J. C. Wenger

Preachers Preaching

It's the preachers in the pulpit, though, who tend to have the most and the funniest stories told about them—as if their high calling and spiritual and moral pretensions need to be squared with the realities of daily life. In the sequence that follows, John W. Hess (1884-1958) was an evangelist and pastor in Missouri, Iowa and Pennsylvania. Nelson Litwiller (1898-1986) was a missionary to Argentina. And Don Jacobs is a retired missionary to East Africa who worked for the Eastern Board of Missions in Harrisonburg, Virginia.

John W. Hess was always bothered by people who would doze off in the congregation. He said he was preaching one time and some farmer was in the congregation who had a hard day and he dozed off. Suddenly he hears John preaching—and John would get quite loud sometimes—and the man yells out, "I'll give forty dollars for the spotted cow!"

The singsong nature of early Mennonite preaching may account for the sleepy man's sense that he is in an auction rather than a church service.

One Sunday morning Nelson Litwiller was given five minutes to speak. (I understand usually you could expect him to go beyond that limit.) Anyway, he stood up and said,

"The Holy Spirit and I are going to have trouble staying within five minutes." And a voice in the bench behind mine [Carl Kreider 1914-2002] said, "Let's not blame it on the Holy Spirit!"

This happened in Houston just a few weeks before the 1980 election. Don Jacobs was preaching in one of these big Presbyterian churches, and his message was Christ riding through Jerusalem on the donkey. It was a big church and they had two services. And after the message the members shook hands with him and one of them said, "You know, it was a good message, but you give the one party the whole attention here [i.e., donkey as symbol of Democratic Party]. You know, some of us down here are Republicans." In the next service Don preached the same message and said someone had commented on his other message—about the donkey—saying he should give both parties equal recognition. So Don said he would just stick with the Bible terms and say "he rode him on an ass" and cover both parties. Don Jacobs was serious until the crowd burst out laughing, and all of a sudden it struck him and then he laughed, too.

Editors Editing

Daniel Kauffman (1865-1944) was a very conservative, influential writer and editor at the Mennonite Publishing House in Scottdale, Pennsylvania. Of his many books, *Doctrines of the Bible* (1928) became a kind of manual for conservative Mennonite thinking and practices, including clothing regulations. J. J. Hostetler (1905-2002) was an editor at the publishing house.

In the days when Mennonite men were supposed to wear flat-topped hats, J. J. [Hostetler] wore a crease in the top of his. Daniel Kauffman obviously did not like this, but said nothing. However, in a Gospel Herald editorial later on, Daniel Kauffman said that clothes should fit the shape of our bodies. So we should wear creases in hats only if we have creases in our heads.

C. F. Yake (1889-1974) also lived in Scottdale, Pennsylvania, and edited *Words of Cheer*, for children, as well as other publications. He is remembered as a lovable, eccentric person:

> C. F. Yake once—and often—had a hard day at the office, dictating letters to his secretary at the Publishing House in Scottdale. Once arrived at home in the evening, he led his family in grace at the supper table, saying: "Our kind Heavenly Father, we thank you for the many blessings showered upon us. ... Period. New paragraph."
> —John L. Ruth

The Miller Family

A series of linked stories are told about a prominent Miller family from rural Middlebury, Indiana. Daniel D. ("D.D.") Miller (1864-1955) was an influential bishop in Indiana-Michigan conference during a time of great controversy over the relative merits of modernism or fundamentalism in interpreting scripture and establishing church polity. His son Orie. O. ("O.O.") Miller (1892-1977) became executive secretary of the Mennonite Central Committee from 1935-1958. Ernest. E. ("E.E.") Miller (1893-1975), his other son, became president of Goshen College from 1939-54.

A story about D. D. Miller shows him at his less than upright, nonresistant best. His actions lead to tragedy for another farmer and create an *etiological*, or origins, legend about how a present-day phenomenon came to be.

When the State of Indiana wanted to rebuild U.S. 20 south of Middlebury, they wanted it to follow the foot of the hill and curve north, following the valley and crossing SR 13 closer to Middlebury. That of course would have taken a huge corner off of D.D.'s farm. Whenever the surveyors came and drove in the stakes to mark the route, D. D. went out and pulled them up. Finally, the chief engineer in Indianapolis said he gives up; he had never run into such stubborn opposition before. So he had his engineers keep 20 going west beyond highway 13, then curve north to meet the highway at the point where Essen Haus Restaurant now stands. But that emasculated another farmer's farm. That man's reaction was to slash his wrists [but not take his life].

D. D. Miller's son Orie became so influential in Mennonite institutional affairs, especially the Mennonite Central Committee, that people who worked with him claimed that he wrote the minutes of committee meetings before he came to them. He once expressed that self-confidence as a child, only to be quickly corrected by his father:

When Orie O. Miller was a boy on the farm in Indiana, one day he found a bucket of paint and proceeded to paint, in large letters, his initials on the side of the barn: "O. O. Miller." His father didn't notice until he was working in the field, looked at the barn from a distance, and saw it. "Only Old Mush," was all he said, and he drove on.
—John L. Ruth

About D. D. Miller's other son, E. E. Miller, another story is told that reflects upon both father and son.

Ernest E. Miller told the following story in a psychology class setting. His father [D. D. Miller] had been a well known church leader and evangelist of two generations ago. He often was absent from home for 4-6 weeks at a time. When he got back home he was keyed up, tense, and needed a way to unwind. He would kick the horses a lot—in their bellies. Someone asked Mrs.[Ruth Blosser 1893-1977] Miller what Ernest does to unwind. She replied that Ernest is like his father, but he doesn't have horses.

John Howard Yoder

John Howard Yoder (1927-1997) dominated American Mennonite thought and attention in the late twentieth century, as O. O. Miller, Harold Bender and J. C. Wenger had done following World War 2. Yoder, who first taught at Associated Mennonite Biblical Seminaries (now Anabaptist Mennonite Seminary) and later at the University of Notre Dame, became the most important Anabaptist-Mennonite theologian and ethicist. His influence reached far beyond Mennonite circles, and "Yoderian" thinking continues to influence theologians such as Stanley Hauerwas of Duke University, Christopher Rowland of Oxford and James William McClendon, Jr. of Fuller Theological Seminary. As with many academic heroes, Yoder's personal eccentricities and intellectual genius are captured in the many stories that still circulate about him.

> Once John decided to learn Hebrew. So he took Hebrew language books into his study and locked the door. He emerged a week later with the ability to read Hebrew fluently.
>
> In 1970 John flew to Buenos Aires, Argentina, for a year of teaching in an evangelical theology faculty there. When he boarded the plane he was not able to speak any Spanish, but

he did take along Spanish books to teach himself enroute. His first lecture at the seminary was scheduled for the first day after his arrival. He gave it in Spanish, but with great difficulty, requiring the help of an English-Spanish dictionary. Two days later, at his second lecture, he spoke more ably, although still with some struggle. But by the end of his first week there, he was able to speak Spanish nearly fluently and had no more problems communicating with his students.

One day John Howard Yoder went into Provident Bookstore in downtown Goshen and bought a book. He paid for it and began reading it immediately, while he walked back to Goshen College. He read it all the way to the college. Upon reaching the campus, he realized that he had left his car parked outside the bookstore, so he started the long trek back, reading his book all the way. By the time he reached the bookstore, he had finished the book, so he asked Marvin Musser [the manager] for a refund. Musser refused the request.

When a student at Goshen College, John was walking on the sidewalk along a street where workers were cleaning up after just pouring a new section of sidewalk. As he walked he was deeply occupied reading a book in his hands. Therefore he did not see the freshly poured cement in front of him. He tripped over the forms and fell in, book and all. Without appearing to be hurt seriously, he picked himself up, brushed the cement off of his book, and continued walking down the sidewalk—still reading—as if nothing had happened. Another narrator: I heard that he finished the paragraph before he got up. Another narrator:

And he lay on the ground till he got to the end of a page—flipped a page—and then got up and walked on.

Similar stories are told about Irvin. B. Horst (1915-2011) at Eastern Mennonite College (now University), as well as other Mennonite intellectuals.

John, the story that I first heard attached to your name was on the occasion of dropping by on your first week in Basel to meet Dr. [Karl] Barth [1886-1968]. And his wife answered the door and said that he was in the garden, and you proceeded to identify plants along the way—in Latin. And by the time you reached the far end, she introduced you to him as a good friend.

Yoder replied to the narrator, who was his colleague, saying he never saw his mentor Barth in the garden.

[Yoder and Barth] got into a debate on nonresistance, just between the two of them, and Yoder really had Barth on the defensive during the debate.

While at a party, the host asked John whether he wanted coffee. When he said yes, the host showed him the hot water, mugs, and freeze-dried coffee, expecting him to make it to suit his own taste. Much to the host's astonishment, however, John picked up the coffee jar and a spoon, and began to eat the crystals by the spoonful. He ate half the jar before he stopped.

His students also remember that Yoder studied while standing up at a desk; slept only four hours a night, then got up and read; and kept in his office a plastic bleach jar filled with cold liquid coffee, from which he sipped from time to time. Following his death, information about sexual abuse by Yoder emerged, causing much discussion and controversy in the Mennonite community. However, few anecdotes circulated.

Eastern Mennonite College/University

Three stories deal with church leaders from the Harrisonburg, Virginia, area, where Eastern Mennonite University is located. John R. Mumaw (1904-1993) was president of Eastern Mennonite College from 1948-65. Charles B. Hostetter (1916-1997) became the popular preacher on "The Mennonite Hour," a radio program broadcast throughout the U.S. in Mennonite communities. J. Mark Stauffer (1918-2004) was professor of music at EMC and influential in Mennonite church music along the eastern seaboard.

> At Eastern Mennonite [University] the most commonly told story has been verified by John R. Mumaw, I understand. He was sent to EMC by his parents as an angry, rebellious young man, and came down by the train, which went into Elkton. They would arrive in Elkton and then phone to the college to have someone come over and pick them up. He was thoroughly resenting this whole process, as he was sent down there to be reformed. When he phoned the college, they sent C. K. Lehman [1895-1980] over to pick him up. And C. K. Lehman asked if there's this Brother John R. Mumaw here. And they said, "Oh, yes, he was in here a moment ago. He's around behind." And Lehman walked around behind and he found him standing out there smoking a cigar. The man inside had said, "Yes, I think that's the young man that asked how you get to the damn Mennonite college."

> The same is true for Charlie Hostetter, who was transferred to EMC as a wrestler from Penn State. And he said he had just snuffed out his cigarette right down below where the chapel now stands, walked up front, and C. K. Lehman, who was the dean, met him and took him in to register him. Of course, as he met him, the first thing Lehman did was gave him a great, brotherly kiss, which you did with all incoming students in those days when you were the dean. And Charlie said he held his breath because, he said, "I know I must've smelled enough of tobacco to knock people over." But C. K. Lehman gave him the kiss and took him right on in—registered him.

Both of these stories offer the thrill of observing something scandalous in the histories of men who eventually became moral and spiritual pillars of the church. Smoking and saying "damn" may be petty sins for prodigal sons, but they are enough to give these leaders the necessary credentials of being truly converted, born-again Christians.

J. Mark Stauffer experienced Heaven before he died. Of course, it was a Mennonite heaven, full of the sound of unaccompanied four-part singing:

> I was in one of J. Mark Stauffer's choirs at EMC. He came striding in the room one day and he started out, "I had a dream last night." He said, "I dreamed I died and I was in heaven and I was singing in this huge choir. I looked around. The Lord himself was directing the choir. There were hundreds of sopranos and hundreds of altos and hundreds of tenors. But I was the only bass.... We started singing, and we were singing away and the Lord stopped the choir and said, 'Could we have a little less bass, please?'"

Goshen College

For many years H. S. Bender (1897-1962) was Dean of Goshen College and then President of Goshen Biblical Seminary. One of his students fondly recalls and often repeats this story:

> In class Harold Bender was explaining the Catholic view of Purgatory, and finally Stanley Shenk [1919-2010, later professor of Bible at Goshen College] asked, "Well, now, what about me? What about a Protestant? What would happen to me?" And Harold Bender said, "You go to Hell!"

Like D. D. Miller, Silvanus Yoder (1873-1963) was a farmer near Middlebury, Indiana, and also a part-time solicitor for contributions to Goshen College.

> My dad was soliciting in Illinois for the college—a well-to-do farmer in Illinois. He was in the farmer's barnyard, soliciting, and the farmer was very stubborn. He said, "Oh, I, I, I like to put my money in the [offering] basket on Sunday morning." And somehow Dad got a little exasperated. There was a bushel basket sitting there and he grabbed the bushel basket up and he said, "Well, Brother, here's a basket!" I don't think he got any money.

Russian Mennonites

Three personal legends will acknowledge the rich trove of personal narratives to be found among Mennonites of Dutch-Prussian-Russian ancestry, especially due to their migrations and sufferings during the past 125 years. Frank C. Peters (1920-87) was a leader of the Mennonite Brethren Church in Canada, including as dean of the Mennonite Brethren Bible College in Winnipeg (1957-

65). Peter Dyck (1914-2010) and his wife Elfrieda (1917-2004) did heroic work with MCC following World War 2 in helping Mennonites escape from Eastern Europe, especially Ukraine, and settle in North and South America.

> Frank C. Peters told his congregation one Sunday evening c. 1970 that he had been driving from St. Catherine's to Kitchener on Route 406. He had been preaching at Kitchener and was speeding home. Somewhere past Hamilton he was suddenly stopped by an Ontario Provincial Police officer for speeding. Peters asked, "How did you catch me?" The officer raised a hand, with finger pointed heavenward, and didn't say anything. "Officer," Peters said, "I cannot argue with what comes from above." Then the officer noticed his Bible in the front of the car and let him go.

The story expresses well the ideas that Peters must have treasured as a Mennonite Brethren preacher: the power of the Bible, absolute obedience to the supernatural, and the positive influence of a Christian's testimony.

> The guys in Germany during PAX days [a volunteer reconstruction project] liked peanut butter but they couldn't get peanut butter. It was available in Holland, though, quite cheap. So [on] one trip Peter was taking, he filled up his trunk with peanut butter. And at the Dutch-German border they knew Peter Dyck because was going through all the time. They asked him, "Do you have anything to declare?" And he said, "No. Nothing but a trunk full of peanut butter." And they laughed, and he went on.

Most stories about Peter and Elfrieda Dyck concern the people that he helped escape. Here peanut butter displaces his usual, more precious cargo. But the ambiguous blending of human trickery and divine providence in many stories about Peter Dyck are still present in this more mundane incident.

A cycle of stories about I. M. Friesen, a shadowy figure, circulate among Russian Mennonites, including this legend:

> Irvin M. Friesen went to the sale barn and he bought an animal at the auction sale, and the auctioneer wanted to know what his name was. He says, "I. M. Friesen." Auctioneer says [agitated voice], "I am freezing, too. But, hey, I want your name!"

But exactly who is I. M. Friesen? And is his first name Irvin or Isaac? Although in the history of the large Friesen clan there must have been at least one man with the initials "I. M.," he cannot be recalled as a living person by informants, nor do genealogical records identify him. The best that can be said is that, in the folklore family, he is a first cousin of the equally legendary man from mainstream American folklore, named I. P. Standing.

Strong Men

One type of folk narrative seldom found in Mennonite and Amish circles is the *tall tale*, that is, the usually amusing story that exaggerates human experience or human achievement toward the fantastic. The Mennonite and Amish suspicion of fiction, and preference for legend, may be one reason for that lack. Another might be the traditional Anabaptist emphasis on humility. In the same way that one must not think highly of oneself, so in storytelling one should not make extraordinary claims. The decorum of story-telling complements the decorum of character. But probably the main reason for their scarcity today is that the tall tale is more characteristic of traditional rural culture than of contemporary urbanized culture, which is more likely to express itself through the trickster tale than the tall tale.

Even so, two cycles of stories about very strong men continue to circulate in Mennonite and Amish circles. One has as its hero "Strong" Isaac Kolb (1711-1776), who was a preacher in the Rockhill and Plains congregations in eastern Pennsylvania. The hero of the other cycle is "Strong" or "Strong Arm" Jacob Yoder (1726-1790), an Old Order Amish farmer from the Kishacoquillas Valley ("Big Valley"), Mifflin County, Pennsylvania, near Belleville. The extraordinary strength of both men sometimes expressed itself ambiguously in violence toward other people. Such stories are as close as one will get to finding "The Mennonite Book of War Heroes" mentioned at the beginning of Chapter 1.

> One day, during a barn-raising, Strong Isaac Kolb and others discussed during the noon meal whether it would take one or two teams of horses to pull a certain beam to its location in the barn. After lunch, while the men were chatting on the porch, they saw Strong Isaac walk past, carrying the beam on his shoulder.
>
> Strong Isaac Kolb spent a night at a tavern on his way to somewhere. In the tavern he was taunted by a young man who said, repeatedly, "Isaac Kolb won't fight." Whereupon, Strong Isaac finally went over to him, lifted him up high in his arms and slammed him back down in his chair so hard that it shattered. The young man said, "I'll never torment Isaac Kolb again."

Despite the violence latent in Kolb's behavior in the second story, it was told in 1983 with relish by John E. Lapp (1905-1988), a much revered retired bishop from the Franconia Mennonite Conference, to an assembly of Mennonites in the old Franconia meeting house.

Strong Jacob Yoder excelled in the same kind of hoisting power and sometimes also used it in morally ambiguous ways:

> My uncle's barn gable ends are stones. The top stone they can now measure, they estimate weighs about 300 pounds. The story goes that [Jacob Yoder] put the stone up there himself.
>
> [Strong Jacob Yoder] dismantled a wagon because of a flooded stream and took all the parts across and all the grain sacks across too. And then reassembled [the wagon].
>
> Jacob Yoder was a first-generation immigrant. He would take two 100-pound sacks of wheat to the top of the mill, one on each shoulder, or one under each arm. And as he would go up, someone would reach out through a window on the way up and tweak his beard. And finally he took up only one [bag] and grabbed this guy instead and took him on up.
>
> The way they showed their strength in those days was with wrestling matches. [Jacob Yoder] was the strongest boy in Big Valley and he obviously was the champion. Some boys in Lancaster County heard about Strong Arm Jake and they were sure that they could easily take him on. So they came to Big Valley and were going through the valley and saw a fellow plowing. So they called to him and said, "You know where Strong Arm Jake lives?" The person lifted the plow and said, "Yeah, right over there." They ran back to Lancaster.

The narrative element of a strong man pointing directions by lifting his plow has such a worldwide spread in folk narrative that it has been given its own number—F624.4—in Stith Thompson's magisterial index of folklore motifs, *Motif-Index of Folk-Literature,* 6 vols. (1955-58). That allows us to be a bit skeptical of other awesome elements in these tall tales and to enjoy them more as fiction than history.

William McGrath, the Beachy Amish minister described in Chapter 5, published a kind of official, moralized version of the preceding story (p. 76), which incorporates elements from the other accounts given here. McGrath does not interpret the story as confirming Strong Jake's nonresistance, although some details of his narrative suggest that meaning. Instead, he introduces the story by quoting Psalm 27:1 and 1 John 4:18, both of which emphasize the casting out of fear.

Mennonite Women

To the several stories dealing with tobacco use, cited above, needs to be added the following, which also shows the influence of Mennonite women in church and community affairs—even if they are barely represented in legends in this chapter. Moses Horning (1829-1906) lived in Lancaster County.

> Bishop Moses Horning, when ready to go to the store for groceries, said to his wife, "I have trouble with my stomach. I guess I will get me a pack of chewing tobacco. Maybe that will help." His wife said, "I have the same trouble. Would you bring me a pack also?" So Mose went to the store and came home without any tobacco.

A more farcical, cynical view of the power of a Mennonite woman comes from the Bucks County Mennonite community and involves a married couple, Henry and Sallie Moyer, whose life dates cannot be documented.

Henry Moyer was a sort of an ornery kid and an even more ornery young man. He got the name of "Devil Hen," for Hen—Henry, you know. He married Sallie and they lived on what is presently known as Pearl Buck's farm and they had a rocky marriage. She didn't like him and he didn't like her. Everyone knew it. So when they had their bedroom downstairs, he was in bed sleeping. She took her rope and tied it around his neck and put it up through the hole where the stovepipe goes, and she went up there. In the meantime, he knew what she had done. So he took the rope and tied it to a stove. She went upstairs and pulled on the rope and she pulled the stove up against the ceiling and she thought she was pulling him. She yelled out of the window and yelled, "Fire! Fire!" and then a lot of people came and they saw the stove—and Henry with a grin on his face. This got out in the community. My folks like to tell that story, but, oh, with a great deal of embarrassment.

The narrator insists that the event really occurred, but its farcical, improbable physical battle between the sexes connects it with the *fabliaux* tradition in universal folk literature.

Although Mennonites until very recently have cultivated a separatist stance regarding "the world," the community nevertheless seems to cherish accounts of Mennonites' brush with world-famous people. The first story comes from a Dutch Mennonite family line that first moved to the Danzig area but eventually settled in Ukraine. The second comes from a Swiss-Alsatian Mennonite family connected with Goshen College, in Indiana, which has often hosted prominent international leaders. Both come from women narrators and both concern the woman of the house in her traditional domestic role, serving breakfast:

It's about a woman who was my great-great-great-great grandmother in Russia—four greats. And it's very simple. One morning they woke up and some of the military officers came galloping into their village on horses, very early in the morning, before five, and pounded on their door. They got up and were rather frightened. But the officers just told them the Czar was coming through in an hour and he wanted breakfast. And so that grandmother of mine cooked breakfast and the Czar came and ate in their home and then went on his way.... When my dad told it to us he was sort of proud of the fact that, you know, way back in our ancestry the Czar ate breakfast in one of our homes.

In the early 1960s Clement Atlee [1883-1967], who was a former Prime Minister of Great Britain, was speaking at [Goshen] College. And I'm not sure if he stayed overnight at John Fisher's [1926-2014] home or just had breakfast there, but Pauline cooked porridge for him and served it to him. She said afterward that he told her that this was the best porridge he had had in America. Our family always jokes about that.

Tribute to J. C. Wenger

This scattered gathering of personal legends will close with an inspirational story about John S. Coffman (1848-1899), a native of Virginia, who became the first Mennonite evangelist and, near the end of his life, chair of the board of the Elkhart (Indiana) Institute, which eventually became Goshen College. Coffman deserves much credit for helping make American Mennonites the more dynamic, outward-looking group that they have become today, one century later.

[Coffman] went to Bridgewater Normal [one term in 1875], which is now known as Bridgewater College [in Harrisonburg, Virginia]. The president was a Dr. Bucher. And Coffman would go to him and say, "I really would like such and such a book and I can't afford to buy it."

"Oh," Bucher said, "no problem. I'll just loan you my copy." So he loaned this young man, who was such a worthy young man, by this time married and starting his family and farming a very hilly farm near Mole Hill—that's known to anybody that knows Harrisonburg, Virginia—and he would rest the horses at the end of the row and pull out this book and read a while, and then he'd go on with his work. And then when he was done with the books he took them back to Dr. Bucher and reached for his wallet to pay him. And Bucher said, "Do you think I would take anything from a young man as eager for an education as you are?" And they said John S. Coffman's eyes filled with tears—he was so moved at the kindness of this man.

This story was told to me by John C. Wenger—mentioned recurrently in this book—who was one of the great Mennonite raconteurs of the late twentieth century. Although he appreciated any story for its own sake, he was masterful in using stories from Mennonite experience in his sermons and other public presentations, in order to make his intellectual and emotional points about Mennonite history and beliefs. And to entertain and please his listeners. He dressed and thought conservatively, but his friendly demeanor and his winsome story-telling united all members of his audience, across the divides of Mennonite splinterings. The book concludes with reference to J.C. as a tribute to his respect for and memorable use of Mennonite folk narratives, and his lifelong appreciation for Mennonite folk culture.

· Sources ·

Beck, Ervin. *MennoFolk: Mennonite & Amish Folk Traditions* Scottdale, PA: Herald Press, 2004.

_____. *MennoFolk2: A Sampler of Mennonite & Amish Folklore.* Scottdale, PA: Herald Press, 2005.

_____. "Menno's Children: Tricksters All." *Goshen College Bulletin* (May 1983): 6-7.

_____. "Stories Mennonites Tell." *Gospel Herald* (31 Jan. 1984): 68-71.

Braun, Orlando. "That Mennonite Joke." Docu-Comedy (film). Prairie Boy Productions 2016.

Brednich, Rolf. *Mennonite Folklife and Folklore.* Ottawa: National Museums of Canada, 1977.

Chornoboy, Eleanor Hildebrand. *Faspa with Joy: A Snack of Family Stories Told by Family and Guests.* [Canada: The author], 2007.

Gates, Gary. *How to Speak Dutchified English.* Intercourse, PA: Good Books, 1987.

Good, Merle, Rebecca Good and Kate Good. *Menno-lite: A Humorous Look at Mennonite Life.* Intercourse, PA: Good Books, 2001.

Haas, Craig and Steve Nolt. *The Mennonite Starter Kit: A Handy Guide for the New Mennonite. (Everything They Forgot to Tell You in Church Membership Class!).* Intercourse, PA: Good Books, 1993.

Lesher, Emerson L. *The Muppie Manual: The Mennonite Urban Professional's Handbook for Humility and Success.* Intercourse, PA: Good Books, 1985.

McCabe-Juhnke, John. "Enacting Gemeinde in the Language and Style of Swiss Volhynian Mennonite Storytelling." *Heritage of the Great Plains* 27.2 (Summer 1994): 21-38.

Mumaw, John R. "Mennonite Folklore." *Pennsylvania Folklife* (Spring 1960): 38-40.

Reimer, Al, et al, eds. *A Sackful of Plautdietsch: A Collection of Mennonite Low German Stories and Poems.* Winnipeg: Hyperion Press, 1983.

Schlabach, Kyle. *The Cow in Science Hall: A Collection of Goshen College Folklore.* Goshen, IN: Pinchpenny Press, 1994.

Smith, Elmer Lewis. "Amish Stories." *The Almanac of Pennsylvania Dutch Folklore* (1960): 33-34.

_____, *Pennsylvania Dutch Folklore.* Lebanon, PA: 1960.

Weaver, J. Denny. "Mennonite Symbol Statements." *Shun* (Fall 1983): 28-29.

www.ingramcontent.com/pod-product-compliance
Lightning Source LLC
Chambersburg PA
CBHW030440010526
44118CB00011B/731